Penguin Critical Studies

The Winter's Tale

Christopher Hardman was educated at Pembroke College, Oxford, and is now Senior Lecturer in English at Reading University. His research and publications are mainly in late medieval and Renaissance literature, and especially in Shakespeare's comedies and late plays and in the work of Andrew Marvell. He is also interested in computer assisted editing of literary texts. He is an editor of *Reading Medieval Studies* and joint editor of the New Variorum edition of *The Tempest*.

Penguin Critical Studies
Advisory Editor:
Bryan Loughrey

The Winter's Tale

Christopher Hardman

Penguin Books

PENGUIN BOOKS

Published by the Penguin Group
Penguin Books Ltd, 27 Wrights Lane, London W8 5TZ, England
Penguin Books USA Inc., 375 Hudson Street, New York, New York 10014, USA
Penguin Books Australia Ltd, Ringwood, Victoria, Australia
Penguin Books Canada Ltd, 2801 John Street, Markham, Ontario, Canada L3R 1B4
Penguin Books (NZ) Ltd, 182–190 Wairau Road, Auckland 10, New Zealand

Penguin Books Ltd, Registered Offices: Harmondsworth, Middlesex, England

First published 1988
10 9 8 7 6 5 4 3

Printed in England by Clays Ltd, St Ives plc
Filmset in 9 on 11 pt Monophoto Times

Contents

1: The Structure of the Play
Introductory 1
Freedom and Restraint 2
The Kinds in the Elizabethan and Jacobean Theatre 4
Tragicomedy: Two-part Structure 7
Tragicomedy: the Denouement 13
The Winter's Tale and Comic Form 16
Comedy and Tragicomedy in Shakespeare's Plays 25

2: Shakespeare's Sources for *The Winter's Tale*
Introductory 28
What Shakespeare made of Greene's *Pandosto* 30
Pastoral and Romance 41
Pageants and Masques 47

3: Themes and Ideas in the Play
Introductory 50
Nature and Art 50
Grace 55
Time 59
Forgiveness and Restoration 61
Parents and Children 62
The Faithful Woman 63
Jealousy and Friendship 64
Conclusion 66

4: Character, Speech and Style
Introductory 67
Genres, Style and Characterization 69
The Characters 76

5: *The Winter's Tale* in the Theatre
The Theatre in Shakespeare's Time 94
The Stage History of *The Winter's Tale* 101
The Winter's Tale in the Theatre Today 103

6: Critical Views of the Play
Introductory 111
Parabolic Readings of *The Winter's Tale* 113
Alternative Critical Approaches 116

Bibliography 120

Preface

This book is intended for students studying *The Winter's Tale* for Advanced Level and at University. Consequently it assumes a sound knowledge of the play. While the chapters are arranged in what seemed to be the most sensible order for reading from the beginning to the end, an attempt has been made to make each one fully self-contained, so that any particular topic of interest may be taken as a starting point. There are naturally many instances of interconnection between chapters, and these are pointed out. Whenever a chapter deals with material of a more general kind, relevance to *The Winter's Tale* has always been kept in mind. In the treatment of sources, though the major source is discussed in some detail, the main emphasis is on the use Shakespeare made of his material. The account of critical views on the play and the Bibliography should enable those who are interested in reading further to do so with an idea of where to go and what to expect. Footnotes have been kept to a minimum, and clear, short references are included in the text. Full details of books referred to are to be found in the Bibliography. All quotations from *The Winter's Tale* are taken from The New Penguin Shakespeare edited by Ernest Schanzer, which is recommended.

1. The Structure of the Play

Introductory

The Winter's Tale is one of a group of plays written towards the end of Shakespeare's career, which includes *Pericles*, *Cymbeline* and *The Tempest*. All of them have long been recognized as sharing certain characteristics, and, as a consequence, they have frequently been placed in the same group by critics and given the same label: romances or tragicomedies for example. No doubt Shakespeare's contemporaries would, like us, have often thought of the plays together. Indeed some would have had an opportunity of seeing them and comparing them within a short period: for example Simon Forman saw performances at the Globe theatre of *Cymbeline*, probably between 20 and 30 April 1611, and of *The Winter's Tale* on 15 May 1611, and the first performance of *The Tempest* took place at court on 1 November in the same year. However, there is no evidence that any of them would have gone as far as to consider that they formed, or were part of, a subgenre of their own. Indeed they were not all grouped together in the first collection of Shakespeare's work – *Pericles* does not appear there at all – and this provides us with a timely reminder neither to concentrate solely on the similarities between the four plays and ignore the differences, nor to isolate them from our reading of other plays. A. D. Nuttall's assertion in *Shakespeare: The Winter's Tale* (p. 9) that there is 'a sense in which the last plays of Shakespeare are *sui generis*' is therefore misleading. What even moderately well-educated and well-informed members of Shakespeare's audience would certainly have recognized in each of them was the influence of important current ideas about dramatic form. They would have been able to place the plays in a general theoretical context now unfamiliar to most students, and to see them in relation to the practice of contemporary dramatists. They would not, I think, have treated them as a separate phenomenon. It may therefore help to sketch in very briefly, something of this background before looking in more detail at *The Winter's Tale*.

Freedom and Restraint

When we visit the theatre today to see a modern play we have a general idea what to expect if we are told that it is, for example, a comedy, but we certainly don't have in our minds a series of fixed definitions to measure it against, and we tend to be fairly flexible in our willingness to accept a dramatist's individual interpretation of the form. Most Elizabethan and Jacobean audiences were doubtless no less flexible and tolerant than modern audiences. Certainly the plays themselves frequently did not fit into the strait-jacket of rigid prescriptions, and sometimes not even into quite generally defined categories. It is certainly clear that then, as now, the most popular, and sometimes the best, practitioners did not swallow the precepts of critical theorists whole. However, there can be no doubt that many members of both Elizabethan and Jacobean audiences, and certainly the playwrights themselves, would have remembered quite clear formal definitions of what plays should be like, at least according to the pedagogues, from their grammar-school education. There they would not only have studied the Roman dramatists, Plautus and Terence, but would have learned, especially from the latter, about metrics and about the dramatic decorum that affected characters and style, that is, what kind of characters were appropriate to each sort of play and how they should act and speak. They would almost certainly have read Terence in an edition with an introduction and commentary which would have provided neat, succinct and pithy definitions of what comedy and tragedy were. They might have been aware, too, of more recent writing and controversy about drama. But whether they were or no, much of what it had to say about form was based on classical foundations. The existence of rules and the reverence for classical models did not appear to hamper the creativity of practitioners. Quite the contrary: rules were sometimes followed, but sometimes profitably bent or broken, and on occasions even ignored completely. Their very presence seems now and then to have encouraged, rather than discouraged, invention, and the clash between the order they recommended and the freedom from restraint experienced in vernacular literature produced striking and original works of art as well as jumbles. If the transgression of rules sometimes disturbed formal criticism, at least it does not seem to have much affected the enjoyment of the audience.

Ben Jonson was acutely aware of the artistic dilemma this combination of classical rules and native freedom produced. It emerges in many famous critical remarks, often in the prologues or choruses to his plays, some of which refer directly, and others obliquely, to Shakespeare himself. Jonson clearly despised outrageous romantic plots in which 'a child could be born in a play, and grow up to a man, i'the first scene, before he went off the stage: and then after to come forth a squire, and be made a knight: and that knight to travel between the acts, and do wonders i'the Holy Land or elsewhere; kill Paynims, wild boars, dun cows, and other monsters; beget him a reputation, and marry an emperor's daughter for his mistress: convert her father's country: and at last come home lame, and all-to-be-laden with miracles' (*The Magnetic Lady*, Act I, Chorus). He disliked 'tales, tempests, and such like drolleries' (*Bartholomew Fair*, Prologue), and the contemporary predilection for the 'mouldy tale' like *Pericles*, 'servant-monsters' like Caliban, and the inventiveness which could provide Bohemia with a convenient seacoast. For Jonson the truly great comic writer kept the essential rules:

> The laws of time, place, persons he observeth,
> From no needful rule he swerveth;
> (*Volpone*, Prologue 31–2)

The proper argument for comedy was not for 'a duke to be in love with a countess, and that countess to be in love with the duke's son and the son to love the lady's waiting-maid: some such cross wooing, with a clown to their serving-man' (*Every Man Out Of His Humour*, III.6.195 ff.), which sounds rather like the involved plots of the kind of romantic comedy Shakespeare wrote; rather it should 'show an image of the times', imitate 'deeds, and language such as men do use' (*Every Man In His Humour*, Prologue 21), 'sport with human follies' (*E.M.I.H.H.* Prologue 24), and be 'accommodated to the correction of manners' (*E.M.O.O.H.H.* III.6.208–209). Yet in his commendatory poem in the First Folio he speaks of his admiration for Shakespeare, honouring him 'as much as any', and, praising his art, he esteems him as the equal of the best classical models, of Aeschylus, Sophocles and Euripides in tragedy, and of Aristophanes, Plautus and Terence in comedy. He could see in Shakespeare an unclassical lack of restraint and yet recognize that he did owe something to the ancients and to the classical tradition as well, and further, that by some strange alchemy his genius had combined these elements and raised him to a stature equalling that of the most admired dramatists. The duality of his experience of, and attitude towards, the work of his great contemporary was doubtless echoed in his thoughts and feelings about his own work. Despite his repeated protestations of admiration for classical order, his adherence to tradition, and fidelity to ancient models, there can be no doubt of his own debt to native tradition. And further, whatever he wrote or said, his great comedies are really no closer to Plautus and Terence than are Shakespeare's.

The Kinds in the Elizabethan and Jacobean Theatre

Since there is a great deal of critical discussion about the form of *The Winter's Tale* – it is often called a tragicomedy, for example, something of a hybrid form, and one which is rather tricky to define – it is particularly necessary for the student of this play to sort out, at least in an elementary fashion, the theory of the 'kinds' in contemporary dramatic practice (this is now usually called the division into genres).

When Shakespeare's friends and fellow actors John Heminge and Henry Condell compiled the first collected edition of his works in 1623, they were rather conservative and simply divided the plays in this splendid memorial volume, now known as the First Folio, into the three principal genres recognized in the drama of their time by serious criticism: comedy, history and tragedy, and proudly advertised their author's versatility on the title page. They did not have categories like tragicomedy or romance, and so *The Tempest* and *The Winter's Tale* were placed with the comedies, and *Cymbeline* with the tragedies. Of course we have no idea whether Heminge and Condell would have grouped them together had they chosen to use a wider range of categories. Though we may guess, we do not know where they would have placed *Pericles*. Indeed we do not know for certain why they left it out. If Heminge and Condell were content with, or prepared to make do with, three kinds of play, their contemporaries were, however, frequently much less satisfied with such straightforward categories for containing and describing the variety of dramatists' practice, and so these were continually multiplied and the boundaries between them blurred. There was already a genuine critically approved, overlapping relationship between tragedy and history, deriving ultimately from the Aristotelian tradition that tragedy should be, or should seem to be, historical. Both treated of affairs of state and the public lives of great men, and the elevation of historical figures frequently terminated in the disastrous fall looked for by the tragedians. It was a striking way of presenting Aristotle's principle that a reversal of fortune from good to bad makes the best tragedy. The fall of a king seemed particularly appropriate not just because the dramatic effect is greater – the higher they are the harder they fall – nor because an audience is more disturbed when someone who is apparently socially and materially secure proves to be as subject to the changeable nature of this transitory world as anyone else, but also because Renaissance tradition interpreted in social terms Aristotle's view that tragedy should deal with men who were better (presumably meaning nobler in spirit, more magnanimous) than those who usually surround us: only kings, or at the least aristocrats or great heroes, can be moved by intense emotions such as are unknown to ordinary mortals, and they alone can perform deeds, or even crimes of great passion. In both history and tragedy the protagonist may be wholly or partly responsible for his own fate, or the victim of the machinations of others. He may respond stoically to his predicament, or he may struggle, or even rage heroically, if futilely, against the afflictions of his persecutors, or against the nature of the human condition itself. The association of tragedy with history is almost invariable in the Folio. Nearly all of the tragedies may be described as histories in one way or another. Their material is drawn from the matter of Troy, and from Roman, British and Scottish history, with only *Romeo and Juliet* and *Othello* deriving from Italian stories. Amongst the histories both *Richard II* and *Richard III* are tragedies which find a place as part of the sequence of English history plays, though they would have been just as much at home with the Roman tragical histories in the tragedy section.

This overlap between genres is simple and entirely rational, but things were often far less comprehensible. Many of Shakespeare's contemporaries must have been amused by the super-subtle hair-splitting of those critics quick to spot and define every dramatic hybrid. The most familiar example to the modern student of the drama is Polonius's description of the kind of plays to be found in the repertoire of the company of players which visits Elsinore: 'tragedy, comedy, history, pastoral, pastoral-comical, historical-pastoral, tragical-historical, tragical-comical-historical-pastoral'. Though this is, of course, an exaggeration, mixtures of elements which the strict critic would have considered proper to only one of the kinds did abound. The serious historical, or pseudo-historical, public affairs, the elevated social rank of the *dramatis personae* and the disastrous conclusion usually found in tragedy, were often diluted by the more obvious fictionality, the happy ending, the private affairs, the greater part played by those of lower social rank (the middle classes and servants, for example, people Renaissance critics would have identified as belonging to that Aristotelian category of those meaner in spirit than the persons of tragedy) – features all commonly found in comedy. There was ample precedent for much of this in native tradition which had always adhered less strictly to generic rules. Fools, clowns, drunken porters and grave-diggers in the tragedies look back to the merry devils of the Middle Ages, to the figure of the Vice, a strange combination of the sinister tempter and the comedian appearing, in Tudor Morality plays, and to episodes like the farcical parody of the nativity in the Wakefield *Second Shepherds' Play*, in which a stolen sheep is hidden in a cradle. Sidney referred to this mixing of 'hornpipes and funerals' as producing the kind of mongrel tragicomedy, which was as much an anathema to traditionalists with a classical background as was the grafting practised by the horticulturalist to Perdita. Of course comedies, too, are often mingled with solemn matter, and the darker and more problematic side of Shakespeare's comedies has received considerable critical attention.

However, sometimes the mixture was more radical than, say, the intrusion of a drunken porter in *Macbeth*, and a play which seems to be moving towards disaster somehow ends happily. The seriousness with which one takes the threat that all will not be well varies from play to play and often, indeed, from production to production. Sometimes we are very clearly in a comic world and are confident that its harmonies will prevail, while at other times our uncertainty is disturbing. These two effects may be experienced by comparing *The Winter's Tale* and *Much Ado About Nothing*, for example, and we will return to this later in the chapter. In *The Winter's Tale* we find that the initial confusions with which comedy generally begins have developed into more extensive, darker and more threatening episodes worthy to be called tragicomedy. By the end of the first decade of the sixteenth century, tragicomedy's claim to be an independent dramatic form had been argued over for some years on the Continent, and it was gradually establishing itself as a separate form alongside tragedy and comedy, despite the opposition of more traditional critics; and a link was being established between Continental dramatic theory and English practice and experiment. In the Folio edition of Jonson's works which appeared in 1616, the figure of Tragicomedy stands prominently on the title page beside those of Tragedy and Comedy, dressed in a combination of their attributes as befits a hybrid. She wears the cloak, crown and sceptre appropriate to a representation of Tragedy, indicating the customary royalty and power of the protagonist, while her dress is borrowed from Comedy as are her low shoes, the sock (*soccus*), worn by Athenian actors for comedy, in contrast to the thick-soled boot, the buskin, worn for tragedy. The figure and the Latin inscription below suggest that by 1616 there was at least a serious attempt to treat tragicomedy as a separate and respectable dramatic form.[1]

1. The inscription comes from Horace's *Ars Poetica* (92) where, writing about the distinction between tragedy and comedy, he asks that each kind of play should keep its place in the proper category. Putting this line beneath such a prominent representation of tragicomedy suggests that by 1611 it too was thought to be a properly established dramatic form, just like tragedy and comedy.

Tragicomedy: Two-part Structure

Let us begin our examination of the structure of *The Winter's Tale* by looking at it in the light of some definitions and examples. It may be said first of all that the structure of the play accords very well with what must be the simplest definition of tragicomedy there is, offered by one of Shakespeare's contemporaries, John Florio. It was, he wrote, 'half a tragedy and half a comedy' (*World of Words*, 1598). This certainly fits *The Winter's Tale* better than the best known and most often quoted definition of the form in English by Shakespeare's colleague and collaborator, John Fletcher, which prefaces his play *the Faithful Shepherdess* (1610). In his play and in his description of tragicomedy Fletcher followed G. B. Guarini, the leading apologist for the tragicomic form in Europe, and the author of *Il Pastor Fido* (*The Faithful Shepherd*) the most famous pastoral exemplar of the kind. Fletcher wrote:

> A tragicomedy is not so called in respect of mirth and killing, but in respect it wants deaths, which is enough to make it no tragedy, yet brings some near it, which is enough to make it no comedy, which must be a representation of familiar people, with such kind of trouble as no life be questioned; so that a god is as lawful in this as in tragedy and mean people as in comedy.

This won't really quite do either for Shakespeare's so-called tragicomedies – for example people do die in *The Winter's Tale* – or for his comedies, which are full of gentlemen, lords, dukes and even princes. By comparison with the many rather more sophisticated and subtle definitions of the kind to be found in the writings of Italian critics, Fletcher's definition is rather elementary, yet like them all it suggests a blending of two kinds. In *The Winter's Tale* Shakespeare seems to be determined not to blend elements from comedy and tragedy, not to make the transition from one to the other particularly easy. Instead, he emphasizes the two-part construction of the play and a juxtapositioning of two comparatively unmodified dramatic kinds. Years ago a critic, unconsciously echoing Florio's definition, referred to the structure of the play as a diptych, one part of which was tragedy and the other part comedy. There can be no doubt that had Shakespeare wished, had he thought it appropriate to his purpose, he could have followed the recommended Italian practice. But for the moment let us simply look at what he chose to do and then look for a plausible explanation for his decision.

At the very beginning of this chapter, I mentioned that Shakespeare and his contemporaries would most probably have studied classical drama by reading Terence in an edition with an introductory essay and annotations giving considerable space to an analysis of dramatic structure. The introduction in this school edition is an essay, or rather two essays put together, by the fourth-century critics, Evanthius and Donatus, who had inherited the traditions of Aristotelian criticism, setting out very clear definitions of comedy and tragedy. As it happens the definitions of the two separate kinds describe the two parts of *The Winter's Tale* very well. The essay reiterates the principle, which Aristotle had laid down, that tragedy should give the impression of being based on an historical story, if indeed it was not actually history, and should be about the doings of those who live at court. The first part of the play with its presentation of the court, its attention to the diplomatic as well as the personal relations between monarchs seems to fit quite well. The second part of the play seems, as Donatus suggests all comedies should be, to be more obviously fictitious: it is set in the literary world of pastoral, and is peopled with humble country dwellers instead of courtiers. Shakespeare no doubt made these shepherds to fit the contemporary fashion for pastoral comedy and tragicomedy, even introducing a dance of satyrs to the country festivities. This was particularly apposite for the satyr had very quickly become a familiar companion of the shepherd in tragicomedy, so much so that by 1616 the two already appear together as companions of the figure of Tragicomedy on the engraved title-page of the Folio edition of Jonson's *Works*. The fact that the principals are not really shepherds, and that the comic part ends up moving from the countryside to the court would not have worried Shakespeare's audience, for this was commonly the case in contemporary pastoral and comedy. There are also stock comic figures like the Shepherd and the Clown, and the young lovers Perdita and Florizel.[1] If, in the first part of the play, the threat to life and happiness seems to be, and actually is, substantial, in the second part the dangers do not appear insurmountable and the outcome promises to be happy.

Another fourth-century critic gave what proves to be a very good description of the difference between the two parts of the play when

1. These names were invented by Shakespeare and not adopted from his major source *Pandosto* (see Chapter Two). Perdita's name has a meaning (a lost girl) just as Donatus says names of comic characters should, and Florizel's name may well come from a pastoral episode in a celebrated romance, *Amadis de Grecia*, a continuation of *Amadis de Gaule*, where a Florizel falls in love with a shepherdess called Sylvie, disguises himself as a shepherd to be with her, and is known for a time as the Knight of the Shepherdess.

trying to distinguish between tragedy and comedy. He wrote that the one has as its subject grief, exile and death, with every happiness and good fortune turning to misery, while the other is about love affairs, the carrying off of maidens, and the change from sadness to joy: particularly joy in marriage and in the restoration and recognition of long-lost children.

The two parts of *The Winter's Tale* are divided by what is one of the most celebrated scenes in this play and perhaps in Shakespeare's whole work. In Act III, scene 3 the Shepherd and the Clown discover the infant Perdita, and it is this which marks the beginning of the new comic action, just as the death of Antigonus and the sailors marks the end of the tragic action. When Antigonus put down the baby, he noticed the changing weather and observed 'The storm begins' (III.3.48). In his introductory essay Evanthius had remarked that comedy is tempestuous at the start, and that it is the other way about with tragedy: it begins with calm and ends with tempest. Shakespeare seems to have taken this metaphor from a theoretical essay and translated it into actual events on stage. Here, storm and shipwreck conclude the tragic half of the play and open the comic. The idea was to emerge again a little later in *The Tempest*, where the tragic events of the tragicomedy have all taken place before the play begins and are recollected in the course of the play in retrospective narration, or comically recalled in the ludicrous plot devised by Caliban, so that all the tragical part of the tragicomedy is subsumed into a comic structure. The play begins with 'tempest' and 'mutinous winds', and ends with 'calm seas' and 'auspicious gales' (*The Tempest*, II.2.194; V.1.6, 4, 314).

The change from the tragic to the comic mode in *The Winter's Tale* is emphasized in several other ways, and these would have been fairly obvious to a contemporary audience. In romance narratives, there are not infrequently threats from wild beasts and shipwrecks, but these are rarely fatal. Here, by contrast, Antigonus is eaten and the sailors drown. The kind of events one would normally expect to find turning out well in a comic context, like that provided by the second part of the play, surprisingly have outcomes more suited to tragedy. Actually, however, an interesting double effect is produced. In comedies and in romance narratives characters are saved so that they may fulfil their central role in subsequent events. For example, both Viola and Sebastian are saved from drowning in *Twelfth Night*, while in Sir Philip Sidney's *Arcadia*, two princes escape drowning and two princesses are saved from a bear and a lion to marry them and fulfil the oracle. In *The Winter's Tale* Perdita is miraculously threatened by neither storm nor bear, mortal dangers one would have expected more likely to have affected an exposed infant than a courtier and experienced sailors. So it is that the promise of a happy denouement is not at risk here. The familiar incidents have different outcomes for different sets of characters belonging, as it were, to different parts of the action. The dual response is, of course, highlighted by the way in which the events are presented to the audience; the horror of the scene is conveyed by a description from the Clown, the effect of which is to make the audience laugh. Shakespeare seems rather wilfully to be doing just what Sidney objected to in his *Defence of Poesie* by thrusting a clown in at a very inappropriate place. However, when we see how the action proceeds and recall this scene in the light of subsequent events we may well conclude that it is by no means inappropriate. The effect achieved by this is to emphasize both the change of mode and the way in which such a change can be brought about by the manipulation of conventions and the manner of presentation.

It is quite obvious that we are on the boundary between the two parts of the play. The Shepherd's famous words to the Clown: '. . . thou met'st with things dying, I with things new-born' (III.3.109–10), so often linked by critics to the themes of fertility, rebirth and regeneration they have looked for in the play, take on a new importance when we know that they reflect the pattern of one of Evanthius's definitions of the difference between tragedy and comedy. Tragedy, he said, presented the kind of existence we wish to escape, comedy the life to be embraced. The Clown has witnessed death and disaster and the end of the tragic part of the play, while the Shepherd has found new life and with it the beginning of a new comic action. The exchange between the Shepherd and the Clown which takes place just after Antigonus's hurried departure is rather like a new beginning. It reminds us of the last prose conversation we heard, between two courtiers at the beginning of the play. Both conversations are recognizably introductory, and the status of the interlocutors is appropriate to the part of the play they introduce: shepherds introduce comedy, as courtiers introduced tragedy. Guarini had argued that the tone of the opening scene should prepare the audience for the ensuing tragicomedy and signal to it that what follows is not tragedy. His own *Il Pastor Fido* begins with such a scene. He maintained that if one is made aware that tragedy is possible, one should be equally aware that it will not actually happen. It is hard to be sure of that in the first scene of *The Winter's Tale*, for though the courtiers speak of harmony and love between their kings and people, and are sanguine about the promise of the young prince Mamillius, there is no certain indication from the tone that eventually all will turn out well. Guarini reinforced the impression created by his opening scene by interspersing serious and comic scenes throughout; there is nothing of this kind in the first part of *The Winter's Tale*. In the third scene of the third act, however, the tone certainly and clearly becomes comic.

One thing which Shakespeare does not try to do at this point in the play is to conceal the artifice necessary to effect the change of direction. This may well have already been apparent to the audience in the staging of Antigonus's exit. It is a much discussed question as to whether the man-eating bear would have been played by a real animal or by a man in disguise, and whether the effect was intended to be comic or frightening. Sometimes apparently terrifying bears arouse laughter in the theatre and the effect is similar to that of the Clown's comic narrative of horrific events. Modern bears, except in filmed productions where trick photography is possible, are presumably always going to be played by actors. In the 1610 edition of the popular romantic play *Mucedorus*, which was performed at the Globe, the clown runs in terror from a bear: 'O horrible, terrible! Was ever poore Gentleman so scard out of his seaven Senses?' (I.2), and then tries to explain his terror: 'A Bear? nay, sure it cannot be a Bear, but som Divell in a Beares Doublet: for a beare could never have had that agilitie to have frightened me.' No doubt it was indeed an actor playing a bear, though in the play it is supposed to be a real bear, and the audience would have enjoyed this double perspective. A few lines later as the Clown exits backwards so that the bear will not catch him up unawares, the bear enters from the other side and he tumbles over it, surely not something one would be able to get away with very often with a real bear. Whatever the evidence for real bears on the Elizabethan and Jacobean stage, it must surely be the case that any bear tame enough to have been trusted to pursue Antigonus would have been too tame to have created a sufficiently frightening effect: paradoxically an actor in disguise would have almost certainly been more frightening, as the clown in *Mucedorus* observes, so perhaps that is more likely to have been how it was done. The theatre audience may reflect that in this case the real would be less convincing than the artificial.

In the next scene the necessity for artifice is rather different and it is the kind of thing Sidney and like-minded critics deplored: children here grow up and fall in love in a few lines (Sidney had complained if it happened within the space of two hours!). To get over this temporal chasm Shakespeare presents us with a figure of Time. There is no choice between the real and the imitation here, it has to be an actor; but of course a personification appearing on the stage is not really necessary at all, as the passage of sixteen years is conveyed well enough in the adjacent scenes. However, I do not think Time is, as some have suggested, a rather crude interpolation not in Shakespeare's style. The figure speaks in the rude accents and couplets typical of the pageant, one of the least naturalistic of forms, and the effect is to draw our attention once more to something of which we are frequently and increasingly reminded in this play, that we are witnessing a stage performance, that this is not reality but fiction. A series of different kinds of reminders of this at this stage in the play, and reminders which also emphasize that it is art which transforms tragic events into comic events and that our reaction can be manipulated by the artistic treatment the material receives, may be an important pointer to the effect the play has on the audience and the reader.

This crucial central section of the play contains the change from tragedy to comedy. Guarini in *Compendio della poesia tragicomica* (1601) had recommended a careful mixture of the elements of each kind to avoid a clash between them and a straining of plausibility which might result if the change were abrupt and unprepared for. In *The Winter's Tale* the tragic part is unmixed with comedy. Interestingly, Leontes suffers a passion which could have been the subject of either tragedy or comedy. It can lead an Othello to disaster, or many a jealous husband to ridicule, like Kitely in Jonson's *Every Man In His Humour*. An audience is aware of the comic possibilities of jealousy, and consequently all the more aware that the play does not lead in those directions. Further, the play includes real as well as assumed deaths, and this hampers the possibility of a smooth transition from one kind to the other, albeit that the utterance of the oracle makes us look forward to some kind of resolution. Guarini considered that in a tragicomedy the possibility of tragedy should be recognized without the audience really experiencing its effects.

In *The Winter's Tale* tragedy is certainly experienced before it is replaced by comedy, and potentially tragic, rather than actually tragic events are not wholly resolved in a comic conclusion. Nor indeed is the denouement really capable of the rather comfortable interpretation favoured by some critics. Following Cleomenes's opinion, which certainly does not satisfy Leontes, they take the view that the king has 'done enough . . . performed/A saint-like sorrow' and 'paid down/More penitence than done trespass' (V.1. 1 ff.), and go on to propose a pattern of sin, repentance, penitence, forgiveness and restoration. It is no doubt the reflection of that natural desire to find an explicable and coherent pattern in events, and a just distribution of rewards and punishments based on desert. Yet it is a desire which the play does not fulfil. There is in fact no direct connection between the denouement and Leontes's spiritual condition. Whether he deserves an alleviation of his suffering or no, the return of Hermione does not depend upon what he has done, nor on what he has become, but on the return of Perdita. It is a clear example of the discontinuity between the two parts: tragedy is certainly not replaced by comedy because of a gradual and natural change in Leontes's character as he is schooled by the misery of his memories and the self-imposed hardships of the penitent. At this stage it is not necessary to try to explain why this should be, nor to discuss the reaction of the audience to this. We are simply observing a fact about the structure of the play, which distinguishes it from a recommended tragicomic structural method.

Tragicomedy: the Denouement

Guarini's remarks about the way in which the denouement should be handled reflect the same principle, the same desire to blend the parts of the play into a single, unified whole. The conclusion should be striking and should provoke the awe and wonder of the audience, yet for all the appearance of the miraculous and the magical, there has to be an acceptable and logical explanation of the events flowing naturally from what has gone before: there has to be at least the illusion of the realistic. In tragicomedy the sense of the marvellous is often produced by the dramatist's sleight of hand and it frequently involves amazing events, like the discovery of unexpected relationships and the restoration of lost children, which strike one as implausible. However, these things usually do have a 'natural', a possible, even if an extremely unlikely, explanation.

At the end of *The Winter's Tale* the wonder of the audience is aroused not by the sudden discovery of Perdita, and the happy, if unlikely, chance of her relationship with Florizel. This type of amazing concluding revelation is something that one is very often able to guess in other works when one is familiar with the literary type, but here we can predict it right from the beginning of the second half of the play, and Shakespeare has, it would appear, no intention of making the ending surprise us. Of course it amazes the characters in the play because it is a surprise to them. The gentlemen of the court are full of the events and of the reaction to them:

> ... They seemed almost, with staring on one another, to tear the cases of their eyes. There was speech in their dumbness, language in their very gesture ... A notable passion of wonder appeared in them ...
>
> (V.2.11–16)

Such a deal of wonder is broken out within this hour that ballad-makers cannot be able to express it.

(V.2.23–4)

I shall shortly look a little more closely at some other possible reasons for not staging the discovery of Perdita and her restoration to Leontes, but one reason is that it would be no surprise to the audience. The audience is surprised instead by an event which seems to exceed the usual demands on its credulity. We are confronted with what is, at first sight, a great impossibility: a statue comes to life. It frequently reminds critics of masque devices, where one finds apparently magical transformations accompanied by music leading up to a concluding harmony. Shakespeare's debt to the masque form will be examined in the chapter on his transformation of his sources, but what we notice here is that the device is calculated to arouse even greater wonder than the return of Perdita, and once again draws our attention to the use which Shakespeare makes of obvious artifice in this play.

The explanation of what actually happened is, by contrast, less improbable and more 'natural': the concealment of Hermione by Paulina for many years until the return of Perdita. The contrast between what seems to be happening and what we discover has happened is so great that the lesser of two implausibilities is quite readily accepted in the theatre. There is also an interesting structural parallel with those creaking, unsophisticated devices at the centre of the play, the bear and Time. By contrast with them (and no doubt it is intended to benefit by the contrast), the device by which a statue apparently comes to life and the explanation subsequently offered for this are much more acceptable, nearer to the naturalistic; but the illusion is only momentary, and one we are expected first to be deceived by and then made fully aware of. If all the events, no matter how strange, have explanations, an audience is still conscious – even if the thought is not at the front of many minds while watching the concluding scene unfold – that what happens in a play, what one is prepared to accept when judging by the standards of dramatic art, could not be expected to happen in real life. This is something to which we will return later.

Many critics have shared a disapproval of Shakespeare's keeping Hermione's survival a secret from the audience. It is true that this is unusual: we usually have some clues, some chance of guessing or of seeing something of the character who will turn out to be the long-lost relative. Shakespeare is straining to the very limit the rule that everything has to have an explanation which seems plausible, and it is consequently easy not to notice what he does do to prepare us for the explanation, as he does it rather discreetly. It has sometimes been said that the appearance of Hermione to Antigonus was evidence of a version of the play in which the queen did indeed die, as no one in Shakespeare's day would have thought it possible to see the spirit of someone still alive. Actually, sixteenth-century evidence has been accumulated of examples of visions of the living, and there are, of course, instances in life and literature of dreams in which someone living appears with a message for the dreamer. It is therefore not absolutely necessary for Antigonus to conclude that Hermione is dead from his visionary experience, though of course his conclusion seems very natural to the audience, since it accords with what has apparently happened since Antigonus's departure from Sicilia with the infant Perdita. Shakespeare did not, of course, let us see a ghost on stage which, by convention, would have seemed unambiguous proof.

There is a tendency to allow Antigonus's account to strengthen our conviction that Hermione is dead without ever questioning it, or thinking much about what Antigonus actually says. This is, of course, Shakespeare's intention; he has no wish for us to doubt her death. However, on reflection Antigonus is not a very reliable source. Until now he has always been a sceptic when it came to a belief in ghosts. If those who are inclined to disbelieve such visions think they have encountered the object of their scepticism, they are more likely to convince us of its truth than those who are credulous at the outset. This is the effect brought about by Antigonus's vision, though some doubt remains: '. . . if such thing be, thy mother/Appeared to me last night' (III.3.16–17). There is some uncertainty to begin with as to whether he is experiencing a dream or an apparition: 'ne'er was dream/So like a waking' (17–18), and when it has passed he remarks that he thought 'This was so, and no slumber', but goes on: 'Dreams are toys:/Yet for this once, yea superstitiously,/I will be squared by this. I do believe/Hermione hath suffered death' (38–41). There may well be a play on 'superstitiously' here, meaning not only 'punctiliously' – probably the primary meaning – but also having something of the modern meaning – one editor suggests that it means 'against accepted Protestant doctrine' (Arden, III.3.40). Is it all perhaps a warning about the uncertainty of such experiences? Antigonus doesn't believe in ghosts but thinks he sees Hermione's ghost, is convinced he is not dreaming, observes that dreams are toys, but says that he will believe in this dream. He assumes that Hermione has been executed, presumably having been found guilty, and that Perdita is indeed 'the issue/Of King Polixenes' (42–43), and that this is why Apollo wishes the baby to be abandoned in Bohemia. Nothing which Hermione says in his account supports this deduction. We know, of course, that none of it is right because we have heard the oracular utterance of the god and witnessed the consequences. However, this rarely leads anyone to question his conviction that Hermione is dead because we think we have independent evidence. When we look back to this speech from the end of the play we see how careful Shakespeare has been in his uncertain presentation of the vision.

The Winter's Tale and Comic Form

Guarini considered not only how the denouement of a tragicomedy should be handled and a sense of wonder aroused by the skilful dramatist, but also suggested the effect this should have on the audience, and compared it with that produced by tragedy and comedy separately. The emotions aroused in tragedy are pity and terror, and the purgation experienced produces sadness; in comedy he found laughter and consequently relaxation and the dissipation of sadness. In tragicomedy the pathetic is combined with elements of the comic, resulting in the purging of melancholy and a consequent delight, albeit balanced by the gravity usually found in tragedy. Something of this may be seen at the end of *The Winter's Tale*, despite the rather sharp division of the play into two halves and the lack of blending. Different audiences react differently to the conclusion, but it is certain that the happiness occasioned by the union of Perdita and Florizel and the return of Hermione is balanced by the gravity of the memory of what has been lost in the 'wide gap of time'. Some seriously doubt if this allows the full purging of melancholy tragicomedy is supposed to effect. Certainly, as we shall see later, the effect achieved at the end is not comic.

When trying to analyse and describe the structure of the play as a whole some critics have proposed that rather than looking to theories of tragicomedy, which were never very common in England, it should be treated, like other late plays, as a special kind of comedy, as its place in the First Folio and its ultimately comic conclusion suggest. If we compare the structure of *The Winter's Tale* with that of the other comedies, however, we notice that this special variation on the regular genre involves quite a lot of interesting changes even in the second and predominantly comic half of the play, and I shall examine some important examples of these changes below. To begin with we notice that the play employs a typical use of change of place: here it is from court to country and back again. One might compare *A Midsummer Night's Dream*, and *As You Like It* and even *The Tempest* where, although all the play is set on the island, Prospero has been exiled from Milan and it is to Milan that he returns at the end of the play. The alternative world presented in such comedies, be it a forest or an island, or another country, is a place (sometimes dubbed a 'green' or 'natural' world by critics) in which, if confusion is at first compounded, it appears at length to be resolved in preparation for a return to the world from which the characters are fugitives. It is a process which seems to support the view that the structure of comedy is essentially conservative, reasserting (if modifying) the status quo, ending in marriages, social reintegration, and the reaffirmation of traditional hierarchies. If young love wins through against parental or social opposition, the matches which are made are not, in the end, examples of youthful rebellion but prove completely unexceptionable. The pattern has obvious affinities with that to be found in the pastoral tradition where courtiers retire to the country to recreate themselves and find there a perspective which enables them to see their former lives more clearly. However, if the initial impression from the court/country contrast is of an orthodox comic structure, closer examination may make us less sure of its orthodoxy, and a comparison with *A Midsummer Night's Dream* should help us to understand better the structural organization of the *The Winter's Tale*.

First of all the confusions are not sorted out in the central section of the play. If, as is often the case in comedy, the pastoral setting provides an environment in which love develops between members of the younger generation, this is only one part of the complex solution of the action and none of it comes to fruition in Bohemia. The setting is not some kind of resolving 'green world'; Perdita and Florizel in fact take flight from the pastoral world presented there to Sicilia. One might compare the more usual flight of lovers from court or city to the country: for example from Athens to the forest in *A Midsummer Night's Dream*. This is a change of place which usually occurs at the beginning of a comedy, not in the fourth act.

The role of Polixenes as outraged parent is in some ways rather reminiscent of that of Egeus, the father of Hermia, in *A Midsummer Night's Dream*. Perdita as a tiny baby has, of course, already escaped the wrath of her own father, Leontes, and found safety by good fortune in this pastoral fastness. The hostile parent is a recurrent feature in Elizabethan literature, in romance and in drama, especially comedy. Here with Polixenes we may compare not only Egeus, but Baptista in *The Taming of the Shrew*, the Duke in *Two Gentlemen of Verona*, and Shylock in *The Merchant of Venice*. Overcoming the opposition proves to be a test of true love, and sometimes the test is set up by a parent eager to ensure the suitability of his daughter's choice, rather than being an example of simple parental disapproval; this is the case with Prospero in *The Tempest* and, in an interesting variation in *The Merchant of Venice*, even a dead father, through the provisions of his will, is able to establish a test which, despite Portia's initial feelings that her freedom is curtailed, proves to be an infallible method of identifying the suitor she truly loves and who truly loves her. But when Leontes threatens Perdita's life we, the audience, know that he is in deadly earnest. Leontes may deny that he is a tyrant:

> . . . Were I a tyrant,
> Where were her [Paulina's] life? She durst not call me so,
> If she did know me one.
>
> (I I.3.121–3)

Yet none but tyrants seek the lives of innocent babies; it is the action of a Macbeth or a Herod. How can we tell that the threats of an Egeus or a Polixenes are different? To the characters in the play they seem terrible. Indeed it is important that the audience should feel some unease and apprehension. In the second part of *The Winter's Tale* one cannot fail to be reminded of the horror generated earlier on by the apparently inescapable, absolute power of the tyrant, though with Polixenes one does not experience the terror Leontes could inspire. Egeus in *A Midsummer Night's Dream* seeks to 'dispose' of Hermia either to Demetrius or to death, and Theseus offers her the stark choice of marriage, death or 'to abjure/For ever the society of men' (I.1.65). Polixenes threatens to scratch Perdita's beauty with briars and promises a cruel death if she continues to see Florizel, while her father is threatened with hanging, though granted a stay of execution. Polixenes's threats are typical of the man beside himself with rage: he first threatens what he will do on the instant, and then what he will do in time if he is not obeyed. To the audience the gap between sentence, or threat, and execution is one of the things that convinces us that this is different: Leontes dispatches Antigonus to expose the infant Perdita with the utmost expedition, and threatens both him and his wife with death if he fails; Polixenes rushes away in a rage leaving the lovers to decide what to do. Camillo is quick to hint that given time there will be a change in the king:

> . . . Gracious my lord,
> You know your father's temper. At this time
> He will allow no speech – which I do guess

> You do not purpose to him – and as hardly
> Will he endure your sight as yet, I fear.
> Then till the fury of his highness settle
> Come not before him.
>
> (IV.4.463–9)

Even when the prince's proposed course seems desperate to him, Camillo determines to assist and 'Save him from danger' (567). His plan to return to Sicilia with the young lovers so that he can satisfy his own wish to see Leontes again not only reinforces our conviction that all will turn out to be well given time, but clearly suggests that in resolving the lovers' plight, Leontes will find his daughter and Polixenes be reconciled to his former friend. Camillo is playing an apparently similar role to the one he played in the first part of the play. The parallelism is very obvious, but this time he is something of the comic schemer. He tricks both Polixenes and Florizel for his and their advantage, and his deception of Polixenes is intended to be excused by his taking action only when Florizel is already 'irremovable' and 'Resolved for flight' (IV.4.506). In the first part of the play he recognized in his master not simply a loss of temper which would soon settle, as with Polixenes, but rather a man 'in rebellion with himself' who would have his servants similarly unbalanced. Leontes's order to poison Polixenes placed Camillo in an impossible position: 'to do't or no is certain/To me a break-neck' (I.2.362–3). To do the right thing is to be false to his master and to risk mortal danger.

In *A Midsummer Night's Dream* Theseus allows Hermia time to consider her refusal to marry anyone other than Lysander.

> Take time to pause, and by the next new moon –
> The sealing day betwixt my love and me
> For everlasting bond of fellowship –
> Upon that day either prepare to die
> For disobedience to your father's will,
> Or else to wed Demetrius, as he would,
> Or on Diana's altar to protest
> For aye austerity and single life.
>
> (I.1.83–90)

We expect that the interim will somehow provide an answer to the problem, and indeed, within a few lines Hermia and Lysander have hatched a plan to escape the very next night to the house of Lysander's rich and childless aunt, who lives beyond the reach of Athenian law, where they can safely be married. The context, too, prepares the audience for a happy outcome. At the very beginning of the play Theseus sets the tone of nuptial celebration:

> Stir up the Athenian youth to merriments.
> Awake the pert and nimble spirit of mirth.
> Turn melancholy forth to funerals:
> The pale companion is not for our pomp.
> Hippolyta, I wooed thee with my sword,
> And won thy love doing thee injuries;
> But I will wed thee in another key:
> With pomp and triumph, and with revelling.
> (I.1.12–19)

It would be an inappropriate and indecorous accompaniment to a royal wedding, were these young lovers to be separated, and Hermia to accept a loveless match, or death, or perpetual virginity: no one would anticipate it. Similarly in *The Winter's Tale* the pastoral context and the merriment of the feast do not suggest an ominous outcome. In both plays the comic setting is soon further reinforced. In the very next scene of *A Midsummer Night's Dream*, the craftsmen rehearse their play against the wedding celebration. The title is a humorous reminder of the contemporary uncertainty, mentioned before, about how to distinguish one kind of play from another: *'The most lamentable comedy and most cruel death of Pyramus and Thisby'*. The story is of course a warning, albeit treated in the most ludicrous manner, of the terrible disasters which can be caused by confusion and misunderstanding between eloping lovers. It therefore both looks forward to the main action of the play on which it provides a kind of commentary, and also promises that the only tears to be provoked at the concluding marriage celebration will come from laughter.

In *The Winter's Tale* we soon find ourselves witnessing the disguising of Florizel and Perdita in Autolycus's clothes. Disguise is the stuff of comedy and indeed we discover that Autolycus has been disguised all along, for he whips off his beard and pretends to be a courtier to confront the Shepherd and his son. The tone of the whole exchange that follows is not at all serious: 'Seest thou not the air of the court in these enfoldings? Hath not my gait in it the measure of the court? Receives not thy nose court-odour from me?' (IV.4.726–9). Autolycus pretends not to recognize the Shepherd and his son and details the tortures these unfortunates will suffer if they remain to endure the king's wrath. We know, of course, that there is no force behind his account. He begins with punishments which are not completely fantastical (stoning, for example), but his expression already has a tendency to hyperbole: 'the curses he shall have, the tortures he shall feel, will break the back of man, the heart of monster' (IV.4.765–7), and the havoc to be done among his relations – 'those that are germane to him, though removed fifty times, shall all come under the hangman' (IV.4.769–71) – indicates a comic exaggeration. By the time the Clown tentatively asks: 'Has the old man e'er a son, sir, do you hear, an't like you, sir?' (777–8), Autolycus is not to be stopped, and his imagination runs riot in teasing his victim with real relish:

> He has a son: who shall be flayed alive; then 'nointed over with honey, set on the head of a wasp's nest; then stand till he be three-quarters and a dram dead; then recovered again with aqua-vitae or some other hot infusion; then, raw as he is, and in the hottest day prognostication proclaims, shall he be set against a brick wall, the sun looking with a southward eye upon him, where he is to behold him with flies blown to death.
>
> (IV.4.779–87)

Because we know him for what he is and understand the tone of the passage, we can enjoy the pair's excruciating discomfort at these threats. At the beginning of this part of the play the change from tragedy to comedy was in part effected by a comic description of actual horrors: here the comic tone is well established and the comic description is of imagined and fantastic horrors. The scene ends with Autolycus alone, reflecting humorously as he pockets gold for agreeing to conduct the pair to the king, though he is intent on taking them aboard the prince's ship, that even if he 'had a mind to be honest' Fortune would not allow it, for she is always putting the opportunity for ill-gotten gains within his grasp. What a change this is from the dire threats of Polixenes at the heart of the scene! If we did not recognize the disguised king there as a comic figure, the ludicrous parody of the threats he made to Perdita and her father in Autolycus's conversation with the Shepherd and the Clown make sure the audience gets its bearings and is not fearful of the outcome imminent in Sicilia in the final act. The threat to the lovers exists in a sequence of scenes which begins and ends with Autolycus gulling the Clown. At the start Autolycus claims to have been the victim of a robber who has stolen his clothes, hence his disreputable apparel which is used as a ruse to rob his good samaritan. By the end of the sequence he has changed his clothes for the better and his appearance convinces the Clown and his father that he is a courtier, which enables him to take their money once again. This repetition with variation of the same motif at the beginning and end of the sequence clearly establishes the context for the events.

In comedies the harmony of the conclusion usually centres on the younger generation, most often love triumphs, lovers are joined in marriage, families and friends are reunited, and at least the major conflicts involving the principals are resolved. The conclusion of *The Winter's Tale* is arranged in a way which once again slightly upsets our normal expectations. If the comic threat from a disapproving parent, the flight and change of place happen rather late in the action, the resolution of the lovers' problems takes place surprisingly early in the final act, and we are a little surprised, too, not to witness it. At the end of the first scene of Act V everything seems to be prepared for a set-piece revelation and resolution: Perdita and Florizel have had an audience with Leontes and their appearance has reminded him of the children he has lost, Florizel reminded him of his former friendship with Polixenes, and Perdita's beauty brings Hermione to his mind. We have heard of the arrival of Polixenes and Camillo and of the renewed threats to the safety of the Shepherd and the Clown. Leontes promises to be a friend to the lovers' virtuous desires. All this has taken place in the final 109 lines of a scene of 232 lines. The disposition of material and lines in this scene needs to be remembered for it is very carefully planned and we shall have cause to return to it later on.

However, the dramatic denouement we expect does not take place. When the next scene begins we find that suddenly time has passed, Polixenes and Camillo have arrived at the court of Sicilia, the Shepherd's fardel has been opened and his story told, Perdita has been recognized, her mother's death revealed, the kings reconciled, and the fate of Antigonus discovered; and the whole court has eagerly departed to view Paulina's statue of Hermione done by Julio Romano. 'The dignity of this act was worth the audience of kings and princes, for by such it was acted' (77–9). We, too, might have expected to witness it, performed with spectacle and expressed in elevated verse, but we only hear of it in 120 lines of conversation between Autolycus and three gentlemen, which is, as is entirely appropriate for such private exchanges, in prose. Autolycus's presence and the prose take us back to the sequence in Act IV where we noticed his importance in helping to provide the comic context, and there is an appropriateness about his playing a part in the presentation of what seems to be the comic denouement. Typically Autolycus had intended to get the praise for the revelations himself, but had failed to communicate with the prince, who had been not only love-sick but sea-sick on the voyage. The scene ends with another exchange between Autolycus and the Shepherd and the Clown, but this time he does not steal their money: instead, always seeking his own advantage, he seeks to ingratiate himself and win their good report. In a sense it is a reversal of the two earlier scenes where they are cheated, a comic exorcism of their previous losses, for they are now much better off than ever they have been. Of course we cannot expect them to be cured of their naïveté and are amused by the Clown's promise to 'swear to the Prince [Autolycus is] as honest a true fellow as any is in Bohemia' (152–3).

This episode apparently concludes the comic harmony of the denouement. From the lovers it has stretched from the highest to the lowest, from king to clown, and now even to the rogue Autolycus. If Hermione cannot be present she will be remembered in the lifelike statue. But all this is not like a conventional comic conclusion. Not only is it quite briefly narrated and not shown, but the preparation for the denouement and the account of it take up only half of the last act, and are apparently concluded with a scene still to go, which, if it is only to present a visit to a statue, will seem to be rather spun out and not very eventful by comparison with what has been happening off-stage. In the event, of course, the final scene proves to be the most amazing in the play. The usual comic arrangement of harmony amongst the younger generation taking prominence is changed, and the dramatic climax of the play is without doubt the restoration of Hermione and reunion and reconciliation in the older generation, though of course Hermione's reappearance is dependent upon the return of Perdita:

> ... I,
> Knowing by Paulina that the oracle
> Gave hope thou wast in being, have preserved
> Myself to see the issue.
>
> (V.3.125–8)

The audience of comedy is accustomed to a conclusion which frequently involves the union of more than one pair of lovers. Florizel and Perdita are the familiar, almost stereotypical young lovers of comedy. There are no other suitable young couples to join them in their nuptials: no Gratiano and Nerissa, no Oliver and Celia. Leontes and Hermione are in middle age and not at all the traditional romantic lovers. They seem to be more suited to the subsidiary role of reunited parents, as played by Egeon and Emilia in *The Comedy of Errors*, but they are far too important: too much of the play, and especially of the conclusion in which they play the prominent part, depends upon them.

Once again the normal comic pattern is drastically modified. The third pair, Camillo and Paulina, are even more unlikely, but their match strikes most audiences as typical of comedy, a rather light-hearted example of extending the harmony of the conclusion, a piece of tidying up, not intended to make any point or reflect anything about the characters and their feelings. It is a humorous reminder of Paulina's sombre function for most of the play. She has kept alive the memory of her mistress and prevented Leontes from listening to those who argued that political expediency required his remarriage. Indeed Leontes had agreed not to marry except on her instruction, aware that that would not be until his first queen was 'again in breath'. Now the tables are turned and Leontes proposes, now that the apparently impossible has happened, that Paulina should 'a husband take by my consent,/As I by thine a wife' (136–7). The serious is modulated into good humour.

The effect is not entirely dissimilar to the technique Shakespeare had used at the end of *The Merchant of Venice*, where the merry jest of the rings provided a bond story we could laugh at rather than one which threatened death for one of the principal characters and misery for the others. Yet here there is not very much laughter. The characters do not leave the stage speaking of celebrations, of feasting and dancing, and of an ensuing comic harmony, but seeking a place

> . . . where we may leisurely
> Each one demand, and answer to his part
> Perform'd in this wide gap of time, since first
> We were dissever'd.
>
> (V.3.152–5)

If the events of these scenes have secured a better future, Leontes's final words concentrate not on that but on the lost past.

The earliest account of *The Winter's Tale* by Simon Forman is probably most celebrated for its silence about the statue scene and the return of Hermione. Since this is so remarkable and most strikes a contemporary audience, critics have sometimes conjectured that there was an earlier version in which she was not restored. Of course this is possible, but if so the whole of the last act must have been very different, for what we now have has been very carefully disposed to deal with both parts of the denouement. The space given to the account of the more conventional comedy conclusion in the second scene is very similar in length to that of the final scene, given, of course, the difficulty of comparing a verse scene with a prose scene, and a scene with spectacle and music with one of rapid conversational exchanges. The first scene of the act gives, as we have already observed, the last 109 lines to the events which lead to the part of the conclusion concerning Perdita and Florizel. These seem more exciting and important than the recollection of a past which cannot now be redeemed. Yet Shakespeare is careful not to let us forget the past. The first eighty-five lines of the scene are devoted to Leontes' recollection of the perfection of Hermione and his refusal to contemplate remarriage, despite the urging of his courtiers. There follows a section of some forty-seven lines in which a Gentleman announces the arrival of Florizel and Perdita, and in an exchange with Paulina is reproached for forgetting the praise he had given Hermione in speech and verse in the past – 'she had not been/Nor was to be, equalled' (100–101) – now his praise of Perdita's beauty pronounces her 'the rarest of all women' (112). So the scene gives roughly the same time to preparing for each part of the double conclusion, and a section half as long as each of these to an exchange which links them, as they are linked in the narrative: Hermione returning only when Perdita does.

The division of the conclusion into two parts simply repeats a pattern which we find throughout the play. Comic theorists and commentators frequently praised the Roman dramatist Terence for his skilful employment of the double plot in his comedies, but the traditional expectation in comedy is for the plots to be interwoven rather than set end to end as these are. It is not only the different modes, tragedy and comedy, which are distinctly separated, but the narrative material concerning the two generations is kept extraordinarily separate almost to the very end.

Comedy and Tragicomedy in Shakespeare's Plays

By 1611 Shakespeare had already written a number of plays which, while ostensibly comedies, show signs of an interest in tragicomedy. It is evident as early as *The Comedy of Errors*: Egeon, alone, separated from his family and a captive in a hostile city is under sentence of death throughout the action. Although in the confusion and errors which make up the interim we often forget his miserable plight, or in the comic context simply expect his enfranchisement, nonetheless at the end he is brought out for execution and released only when the Duke, amazed by the extraordinary discoveries of the conclusion, does what he had initially maintained was impossible and pardons him. We may notice here that Egeon, like Leontes, is a passive beneficiary of the revelations: nothing they do brings them about yet both have a wife, presumed dead, and a child lost for many years restored to them. The influence of tragicomic elements becomes more obvious as we follow Shakespeare's career and is especially noticeable after 1598. By 1604 in *Measure For Measure* a blend of tragic and comic elements is evident in a structure owing much to developments in tragicomic form. Shakespeare, as we shall see, had already employed this very successfully in *Much Ado About Nothing*; but in *Measure For Measure* the problems were much greater, and some find the solution rather forced. Bradley recognized long ago that the influence of tragicomedy also appeared later in what seems at first sight to be a very unlikely place, *King Lear* (1605).

However, the most interesting example for our purposes is *Much Ado About Nothing*, with a structural pattern which is, in some ways, almost a prototype of *The Winter's Tale*. Claudio has just as little reason for his suspicion as Leontes, though at least he is the victim of the unscrupulous deception of Don John and his cronies, rather than entirely self-deceived. Claudio rejects Hero, who, like Hermione, apparently dies. At the end of the play he accepts on trust the veiled niece of Leonato who turns out to be Hero, just as in *The Winter's Tale* an apparently vivified statue turns out to be Hermione. Both men recognize that they have received more than they deserve. In some ways *Much Ado About Nothing* actually follows the standard tragicomic prescriptions rather more closely than *The Winter's Tale*. The overall comic tone is preserved throughout, the audience knows that Hero is not dead and, even before her cruel rejection in the church, that, albeit with ludicrous slowness and incompetence, the bumbling Dogberry and his companions will reveal the truth. Indeed Dogberry and Verges have already announced the arrest of Conrade and Borachio to Leonato in III.5, but he has not the time to cope with their tediousness as he is in haste to get to the wedding. The rejection scene (IV.1) is followed by Dogberry's comic interrogation of the prisoners, a scenic alternation which reflects Guarini's proposals and his own dramatic practice to make sure the potentially tragic parts are balanced by the comic. Since Leonato's instruction that Dogberry should conduct the interrogation, we have been waiting expectantly for this scene, and waiting for it through a scene of a quite different kind. The audience reaction to IV.1 is naturally tempered by knowing that comedy is soon to follow and that whatever happens in the church, eventually someone more intelligent than Dogberry will question Conrade and Borachio. Of course IV.1 itself is not entirely tragic in content; Hero is, as the audience knows almost at once, still living and the Friar talks of her wedding day being perhaps 'prolong'd' (254) rather than cancelled. However, if she is not in danger of death, interestingly the tragic potential is kept up by Beatrice's injunction to Benedick to 'kill Claudio' (289), and his promise to challenge him. It does not last long, however, for in the very next scene (V.1) Benedick has no sooner left, having made his challenge, than the discovery of the truth begins. In general most audiences do not perceive the threat of death in this play to be anything like as strong as it is even in *The Merchant of Venice*, and certainly not as strong as in *Measure for Measure*.

The predominant effect is comic throughout. The contrast with *The Winter's Tale* is very striking, and even a brief and superficial comparison of the two plays demonstrates how a very similar narrative pattern can be treated in entirely different ways and produce very different effects. It is quite clear that Shakespeare positively eschewed Guarini's recommended practice of blending comic and tragic elements in *The Winter's Tale*, in favour of a sharply divided two-part structure, because he wished to write a very different kind of play. The skill with which he handled the dramatic techniques required to blend these elements in *Much Ado About Nothing* leaves us in no doubt that he was completely conversant with this tragicomic method in practice as well as in theory. But by 1611 it seems that he wanted his audience to notice the marked differences between the two kinds, and rather than gloss over them, or modify them so that they may be integrated one with another, he ensured that the structural arrangement of the play encourages an audience to question the nature of the relationship between them. Perhaps because the juxtaposition is so overtly a matter of artifice, and an artifice positively stressed rather than concealed, we are led to consider more generally the nature and extent of the remedial functions of art, especially here dramatic art, and its relation to reality.

We do not accept the harmonious conclusion of the play as something which one could expect to happen in life. These are the contrived harmonies of fiction: the change from tragedy to comedy can only be effected by dramatic art. The method of juxtaposition which Shakespeare adopts rather than the recommended blending, and the stress upon the unbelievable, almost miraculous nature of the events in the final scenes of the play, makes certain that no member of an audience is deceived into thinking comedy grows naturally from tragedy. In *A Natural Perspective* Northrop Frye remarks perceptively that 'the world we are looking at in the conclusion of *The Winter's Tale* is not an object of belief so much as an imaginative model of desire', for 'the world where this unity can be achieved is clearly not the world of ordinary experience, in which man is an alienated spectator' (p. 117). If this is, to quote Frye again, 'a new and impossible world', we recognize that one of the functions of art is to show us the impossible, to construct imaginative models of the world as we desire it to be rather than as it is, and to sharpen our awareness of reality and of the limitations of the human condition.

2. Shakespeare's Sources for *The Winter's Tale*

Introductory

What is the point of studying Shakespeare's sources for *The Winter's Tale*? The student who asks this question can, perhaps rather surprisingly, find some support for the answer 'not much', even amongst a few of the modern scholars who have devoted time and industry to the activity, one of whom has expressed the rather modest view of their achievements that 'sources throw relatively little light on the finished plays' (K. Muir, *Shakespeare's Sources*, p. 254). An interest in the sources could once have been caricatured, without much fear of contradiction, as a kind of pedantic, dry-as-dust antiquarianism: the mere accumulation of material, some of it of rather doubtful relevance; an activity very different from and inferior to that of the critic. That was certainly the rather superior opinion of some critics at the beginning of the century, and there can be no doubt that many took the economical view that the profit to be gained from source studies was too small to justify the investment. This was, at least partly, the fault of the source hunters themselves, who did not always point out, and perhaps often did not fully appreciate, the relevance of their work to the study of Shakespeare's skill in dramatic composition. Over the years the study of Shakespeare's sources has developed from the noting of parallels with classical, post-classical and contemporary authors, and the general identification and summary of works from which he drew his stories, plots, ideas and characters, into a much more detailed and comprehensive activity incorporating a far wider field.

First of all there is the examination of narrative material. This extends from the study of a specific source-book for the whole of a play, like Robert Greene's *Pandosto* for *The Winter's Tale*, to a source for part of a play, perhaps for a character – Ovid's *Metamorphoses*, for example, for Autolycus – or even for the names of characters – North's translation of Plutarch's *Lives*, for the names of Camillo, Antigonus, Cleomenes and Dion to name but a few – to possible influences, which may often be more convincingly described as parallels or analogues (that is, stories which are very similar but cannot be indubitably connected to our play). This range of material may be illustrated by starting with a reference to the appearance of the bear on stage in *Mucedorus* (see p. 11), and then comparing various encounters with wild beasts in romances.

Then there is the study of what is frequently called tradition. This refers to what Shakespeare inherited from his predecessors, for example what he derived from a genre like romance, not simply in terms of narrative material, but in terms of attitudes, approaches, styles, even sources for imagery and so on. There are traditional literary forms, too, especially dramatic forms, and these are usually investigated in relation to his knowledge and understanding of contemporary ideas and practices relating to them, something which we have already considered in looking at the structure of the play. Any tradition finding its normal expression in literature naturally brings with it what are often referred to as its own conventions. This means the employment of practices, methods, procedures and devices which are accepted by the reader, or in the case of drama by the audience, as part of that particular literary form. In the theatre it may include an unquestioning acceptance of verse speaking, of the use of a chorus or a personification like Time, of the soliloquy, of the unities of action, place and time or, in a play like *The Winter's Tale*, the acceptance of the passing of many years in the space of a few hours.

Sometimes we are encouraged to think about the origins of the plays in terms of underlying patterns perhaps adopted from other plays; sometimes these are quite general and fairly obvious, like the influence of the morality play in Marlowe's *Dr Faustus*, or they may be general but less overt, like the influence of revenge tragedy on *The Tempest*, or more specific, like the imitation at the beginning of *Richard III* of the incident in *Cambises*, where the king's honest brother is betrayed by Ambidexter, the witty double-dealing Vice figure with whom Richard later explicitly compares himself.

Modern source studies – though this may not be quite the right term for the interests which I am now going to refer to – include not only the formal and narrative relations of the text to its progenitors, but also concern themselves with what might be called the environment or context in which the work was produced. This can include not only, for example, the physical constraints of contemporary theatre design, or the organization of theatrical companies, but also the relationship of the artist to his society, to current ideas, beliefs, political and economic circumstances, and so on.

The final justification for all this energetic activity is that it enables us to understand more about Shakespeare's dramatic methods and leads us to ask some of those questions which help us to understand a little better, and interpret more confidently, the plays we are studying. I shall not attempt the task of trying to detail all Shakespeare's modifications to his principal sources. Several very competent and comprehensive studies of this kind already exist to be consulted, and those who would like to try to make their own comparisons and draw their own conclusions will find most of the necessary material readily accessible in modern collections. I intend instead to provide brief summaries where necessary and then select for examination in greater detail some of the more important changes Shakespeare made to the material he used, and to identify some of the influences which affected or which might have affected him, in order to demonstrate the significance of these to our understanding of the play. As one might expect, a major alteration of source material will very probably produce an important episode which will also demand our attention under one or more other headings.

What Shakespeare made of Greene's *Pandosto*

Shakespeare's major source for *The Winter's Tale* was a prose work by Robert Greene called:

> Pandosto. The Triumph of Time. Wherein is discovered by a pleasant Historie, that although by the meanes of sinister fortune, Truth may be concealed yet by Time in spight of fortune it is most manifestly revealed. Pleasant for age to avoyde drowsie thoughtes, profitable for youth to eschue other wanton pastimes, and bringing to both a desired content.

It was first published in 1588 and enjoyed considerable popularity, for there were editions in 1592, 1595, 1607 and after. From the wording of the oracle – 'The king shall live without an heir' (III.2.133–4) – we know that Shakespeare used one of the first three editions, for 'live' was changed to 'die' in the edition of 1607 and in later editions.

Perhaps the first thing that one notices is the difference between the title Greene gave his work and the title Shakespeare chose for his play. As we have seen, *The Winter's Tale* was placed amongst the comedies in the First Folio and the title seems to be appropriate to that kind of play. To begin with, two other plays have seasonal titles: *A Midsummer Night's Dream* and *Twelfth Night*, though of course these refer to festive times, rather than to a season which Shakespeare elsewhere refers to as 'tyrannous' (*Henry IV, Part 2*, I.3.62) and 'sap-consuming' (*The Comedy of Errors*, V.1.311), and full of 'furious . . . rages' (*Cymbeline*, IV.2.260). We therefore place it alongside them while registering a difference, conscious that a play with a title referring to winter may indeed be sadder than their festive titles suggest.

Presumably Shakespeare made a careful and calculated choice when he chose to call his play a tale. By doing so he suggests something rather different from his source. Greene's works usually have titles like the one he gave to *Pandosto*. It is a typical title for a prose romance, and emphasizes that the work blends profit and pleasure and has universal appeal to young and old alike. Shakespeare deliberately avoids encouraging any comparison between his play and such overtly didactic romances (although modern readers and critics go on referring to it as a romance because of the use which is made of romance material) and turns instead to the tale. 'Tale' suggests a fantastic story not to be believed or taken seriously – old tales, as the play tells us, were things to be 'hooted at' (V.3.116–17). To one of Shakespeare's contemporaries a 'winter's tale' would very probably have meant a trifle, a slight and perhaps far-fetched story, long enough and engaging enough to occupy one for a dark winter evening. It may well have included ghosts and the supernatural: Peele writes of 'a merry winters tale' and 'an old wives winters tale' to 'drive away the time' (*Old Wives Tale*, Malone Society (1908), 104 and 109). It is the kind of story to which Lady Macbeth alludes when she speaks of 'A woman's story at a winter's fire,/Authorized by her grandam' (III.4.64–5). In the play itself Mamillius speaks with unconscious irony of sad tales being best for winter, and begins a tale which seems to promise to be as sensational and trivial as one of Autolycus's ballads, and which contrasts sharply with the real sadness of his own predicament.

The use of tale in the title, however, suggests that, despite the apparently wintry nature of the fiction, tragic emotions will not be dominant: a tale cannot be a tragedy. Characters within the play even comment on how the events seem to them to be like those in an 'old tale' (V.2.28 and 59). Many commentators feel that the unlikeliness of the events renders the playgoer more likely to accept them on the principle that truth is stranger than fiction. To say that it is *like* an old tale is to make it plain that it is not one. As Ernest Schanzer put it in his introduction to the New Penguin edition of the play: 'When we introduce some true account with the words "Something quite incredible happened to me the other day", we seek to strengthen our listeners' *belief*, not their disbelief' (p. 8). Yet if this is true it is only true in one sense, in the sense that at that moment we accept what is presented or described as real within the action of the play. In another sense the comparison serves to remind us, and we are quite often reminded of it in this play, that we are seeing something acted on a stage, something which we are never really asked or expected to accept as being a copy of life, even at its most incredible. What we are watching is not being passed off as something that could happen outside a fiction. The power of the work of art both involves us and our emotions, while at the same time requiring us to be able to detach ourselves from the fiction, to stand back and appreciate it as a work of art. Like many things we have noticed already and others we shall notice in the course of this study, the title stresses the fictionality of the story.

When he adapted *Pandosto* Shakespeare left out some of Greene's characters and added others. He also changed their names. No doubt recognizing the romance origins of the story, and perhaps remembering the names and settings he had found when working on *Pericles*, the new names are appropriately mostly Greek. Shakespeare may very well have drawn on North's translation of Plutarch's *Lives* for many of these. It contains the names Camillus, Antigones, Cleomenes, Dion, Archidamus, Autolycus (but see below), Aemylia; there is a Paulinus, a Polixenus and a city called Leontium, which may well have suggested Paulina, Polixenes and Leontes. Plutarch has Hermione as a male name, but Shakespeare may have thought of one of the other female bearers of her name in classical literature. The name Mopsa is transferred from the shepherd's wife in Greene's *Pandosto* to one of the young shepherdesses. Mamillius probably took his name from *Mamillia*, another of Greene's romances; Florizel is the name of the hero in the romance of *Amadis de Grecia*, and Perdita (that which is lost) is a descriptive name formed on the same pattern as Marina in *Pericles* and Miranda in *The Tempest*.

There is no precedent for the character of Paulina in Greene's story, nor for Antigonus, Emilia, Dorcas, Time, nor for various lords, shepherds, shepherdesses, and satyrs. Camillo is a much developed version of Franio, Pandosto's cup-bearer, with some influence from Capnio, Dorastus's servant. The Shepherd's son who is called simply Clown, giving a clear indication of his function in the play, is also entirely Shakespeare's invention. Autolycus too is an addition, his name probably deriving not from North but from Ovid's *Metamorphoses* (XI.359 ff.). Ovid tells how Chione was impregnated first by Apollo as he came from Delphos and then immediately afterwards by Mercury, and bore two sons with different fathers: Philamon and Autolycus, the one a master of honest arts, the other of dishonest ones. Autolycus is the mirror image in the play of all the honest arts, which ultimately brings about the fulfilment of Apollo's oracle (see below, p. 88–9).

Shakespeare made many changes to Greene's narrative, some of which were clearly dictated by the process of transforming a prose narrative into dramatic tragicomedy. He obviously recognized the structural potential inherent in *Pandosto* as well as those pastoral and romantic elements commonly found in contemporary essays in this new and fashionable genre. In Greene's romance, Pandosto, the King of Bohemia falls prey to jealousy which makes him seek to have his friend Egistus, King of Sicily, poisoned, Franio, to whom the order has been given, warns Egistus who escapes. Pandosto's queen, Bellaria, is accused of adultery and of plotting to murder her husband. Her new-born daughter is set adrift in a boat and she is condemned. Apollo's oracle, to whom she had appealed, pronounces her innocent, and her husband, ashamed of his suspicions, seeks her forgiveness and intends to be reconciled with his former friend. At this very time news is brought of the sudden death of Pandosto's only son Garinter and the queen collapses and dies. The king is grief stricken and builds a tomb for them both to which he daily repairs to lament his loss. The scene then changes to Sicily.

In general the first part of Greene's narrative is followed fairly closely, and there are a number of verbal echoes. One change we notice immediately is that Shakespeare's Leontes is King of Sicily, whereas Pandosto was king of Bohemia. The point of this change has been much discussed though it is fair to say that no certain conclusion has been reached. It may be that Shakespeare was exploiting Sicily's reputation for crimes of jealousy and revenge as Bullough in *Narrative and Dramatic Sources of Shakespeare* suggests (vol. 8 p. 125), but of course Sicily was also the cradle of pastoral tradition, so shepherds would have been even more at home there than in Bohemia. Some critics have tried to link Perdita with Proserpina, suggesting that Shakespeare was remembering that Proserpina had been kidnapped from Sicily (Ovid, *Metamorphoses* V) – Perdita refers to the story herself (IV.4.116–18) – and was making a parallel between her disappearance and restoration to her mother Ceres and the disappearance of Perdita and her restoration to Hermione. However, the two stories are not really at all like each other in most respects: Hermione, unlike Ceres does not, and indeed cannot, search for her daughter through the world as she is supposedly dead herself, and Bohemia is the very antithesis of the underworld in which Proserpina is confined, indeed it sounds much more like the traditional account of the fertility of Sicily to which she is restored. If Shakespeare remembered the story here he certainly did not make any serious use of it.

Another significant modification is that early in the play Leontes is rather less attractive than his prototype: he begins worse and improves whereas Pandosto is still subject to destructive passion and vice in the second part of Greene's narrative. Leontes is certainly more rapidly consumed with jealousy, though this may, in part, be attributed to the compression necessary in a dramatization. Though, ostensibly to avoid making a rash judgement, he sends to Apollo himself rather than doing so at the request of his queen, his initial refusal to believe the words of the oracle, which Pandosto had accepted at once, is a clear sign of his rashness and overweening pride. He prefers his own fallible mortal judgement to the oracular utterance of a god. Shakespeare's alteration not only gives special emphasis to the king's tyrannical pride but provides a splendid dramatic climax at the centre of the play. No sooner has Leontes denied the truth of the oracle than a messenger brings news of the death of Mamillius, and Leontes at once concludes that he has angered Apollo and that the heavens strike at his injustice. Then Hermione falls. There is a sense that an irreversible process has begun. A little later in the scene Paulina lists Leontes's offences, building up to this climax:

> . . . The Queen, the Queen,
> The sweet'st, dear'st creature's dead! And vengeance for't
> Not dropped down yet.
>
> (III.2.199–200)

In Greene's work the events are by comparison more loosely organized, there is not the same inevitability, the same rapidity of effect following apparent cause, the same dramatic pace. However, Shakespeare has not only produced a wonderful *coup de théâtre* but presents Leontes very clearly as a tragic figure entirely appropriate in the first half of the play: he makes an error of judgement – here consequent on a moral flaw, jealousy – persists in his fault, wantonly insolent to the god in ignoring his warning, and suffers punishment for it. In Aristotelian terms *hamartia* is followed by *hubris* and then by *nemesis* within a few lines.

Greene's *Pandosto* continues as the new-born princess is cast adrift in a boat and washed ashore in Sicily, there to be found and brought up by a poor shepherd and his wife, who call her Fawnia. She grows up a beautiful shepherdess, and Egistus's son Dorastus falls in love with her, woos her at some length, and finally adopts shepherd's garb in an attempt to win Fawnia. They plan to run away together, but her foster-father, Porrus, concerned lest she should be dishonoured and his family destroyed by an angry Egistus, determines to reveal to the king that she is a foundling. However, he is intercepted and forced aboard the prince's ship along with the lovers. The ship is caught in a storm and driven at length to the coast of Bohemia where, fearing the old hostility between Pandosto and Egistus, Dorastus and Fawnia attempt to conceal their identity until they can go on to Italy. But Pandosto, hearing of Fawnia's beauty and wishing to see her, has them arrested as spies. Dorastus is imprisoned but Fawnia is entertained at court with courtesy and wooed by Pandosto who offers her her lover's freedom if she will grant his desires. Fawnia resists and the king threatens. When Egistus, who has become desperately ill at the loss of his son, discovers their whereabouts he asks for the release of Dorastus and the execution of Fawnia and Porrus. Pandosto, his love turned to disdain, agrees. Porrus threatened by death reveals how he found Fawnia and Pandosto quickly realizes that she is his own daughter. The two kings are reconciled and the marriage of Dorastus and Fawnia is celebrated in Sicily. However, immediately after the ceremony, Pandosto falls into melancholy, dwelling on his many misdeeds and kills himself. Greene's narrative ends quickly with a brief mention of the entombment of Pandosto in Bohemia, where Dorastus ends his own days 'in contented quiet'.

Shakespeare follows Greene in the division of the narrative into two main sections and divides the play at the same point. It is a natural and obvious place to make the break so it is not surprising that they both agree here. The transition between the two parts is, however, handled very differently. This is partly explained, of course, by the differences between a prose narrative and a play, but some of the alterations are indications of very different intentions on the part of the two authors. One cannot easily show on stage an infant alone in a boat adrift on the sea, being cast up in a tempest on a foreign shore, nor the child growing up and becoming a beautiful, admired and modest shepherdess. Shakespeare therefore had to devise some method of handling this. What he did, however, was not quite what one might expect. He invented Antigonus to convey Perdita to Bohemia and then the bear to devour him, and saved Greene's storm to destroy his ship and sailors. It is quite clear that he wanted to draw our attention to what is happening here, packing two devices into one scene when, as Quiller-Couch noticed, one would have done – '. . . why introduce a bear . . . why, in the name of economy, not engulf Antigonus with the rest?' (*The Winter's Tale*, ed. A. T. Quiller-Couch, Cambridge, 1931, p. xx) – and then offering us the Clown's peculiar perspective on the events. If this is not enough he introduces the figure of Time to tell us that sixteen years have passed, Leontes is still shut up in his grief, Polixenes' son is called Florizel, and Perdita has grown up, though all of this could be, and indeed is, conveyed in the following scenes in other ways. I have already discussed the importance and significance of these episodes in the structure of the play and there suggested sources in critical writing, in drama and romance which indicate Shakespeare's wish to make the abrupt change of mode very obvious, and there is no need to repeat it here. However, it is worth remarking that this comparison between Greene and Shakespeare is an object lesson in the way in which a study of sources can teach us to ask important and ultimately revealing questions about a work of art.

One of the striking changes Shakespeare makes to the opening of the second part of the story is the introduction of a shepherd with a son rather than a wife. Greene's treatment of the relationship between Porrus and his wife provided some precedent for comedy: she is characterized by Greene as a termagant who suspects her husband of infidelity when he comes home with the child, 'though wondering that he should be so wanton abroad, sith he was so quiet at home' (p. 174), and takes her cudgel to him. This alteration is ingenious. Shakespeare replaces a very familiar and rather hackneyed comic situation with a very different parent-child relationship from the others in the play. This comic duo, together with a further addition, Autolycus, continues to provide humour throughout the second part of the play and, as I have tried to show in my treatment of the structure of the play, helps to create an unmistakable comic context for the events. This begins with their first conversation, which provides a comic prose opening to the second part, parallel to the courtly prose of Camillo and Archidamus which opens the first part; and continues with the Clown's humorous account of disasters, which emphasizes how the way in which events are treated controls the reaction to them, and so alerts us to the change from the tragic to the comic mode which is taking place here. Otherwise, the Clown has no more substance than comparable characters in Greene.

Shakespeare also omits as not dramatic Greene's rather tedious account of the young lovers' wooing, and jumps straight from the finding of the baby to the full-grown Perdita loved by and in love with Florizel. Another apparently small change, which is nonetheless a very clear indication of Shakespeare's intentions, is the way in which he combines the discovery of the lovers by the prince's father and the threat he makes to their happiness with the shepherds' feast. A comparison with Greene's treatment of the threat is revealing. Egistus only discovers the love affair after the lovers have taken flight from Sicily, and so the threat only comes when they have been arrested by Pandosto, who agrees to a request brought by Egistus's ambassadors to murder Fawnia and Porrus and return Dorastus safely home. Shakespeare's change enables Polixenes to be presented as the threatening father familiar in comedy, as I have already shown, and his distraught behaviour, making first threats of what he will do now, and then what he will do in the future is very different from the cold and impersonal use of the word 'murder' by Egistus's representatives: it plays quite a crucial part in the comic reorganization of the second half.

The major change Shakespeare made to *Pandosto* was to the conclusion. Greene describes Pandosto's suicide as closing up the 'Comedie with a Tragicall stratageme' (p. 199). He had only a few lines earlier referred to the discovery of the lost princess as a 'comicall event' or outcome. Shakespeare rejects the tragical stratagem and adds a further comical one, the amazing episode of the restoration of Hermione in the statue scene. The effect of this actually brings the play nearer to the world of traditional romance in terms both of what happens and how it happens, as Schanzer observed (Penguin edition, p. 16). It also gives it the kind of tragicomic conclusion with a happy ending for all. How to give a play a comic resolution, when principal figures had behaved especially badly was, in fact, something of a problem for critics and dramatists, and one of the ways was to have a double ending which was happy for the virtuous and reformed, and which punished the vicious. This is what Greene did and what Shakespeare eschewed. Shakespeare must certainly have felt, as does the modern reader, that the suicide of Pandosto is rather hurriedly dealt with at the end of the story and spoils the marriage festivities and the reconciliation between friends: the decorum is questionable.

However, there were other compelling reasons for his wish to present an ending informed by untainted reconciliation and forgiveness. As has already been suggested in the chapter on the structure of the play, Shakespeare wished the tragic mode to appear to be completely replaced by the comic. The complexity of response he sought for the end of his play was to depend not on a moralistic distribution of rewards and punishments, but on the discrepancy between an image of scarcely credible joy, and the audience's awareness that such an image can only be created by art and does not reflect likely events in life. Greene's Pandosto had of course lusted after Fawnia, had sought to compel her to give way to his advances, and had, when rejected, been prepared to murder her. We tend to forget his repentance in the first half of the story and indeed Greene makes nothing of it at this stage. For Greene to have presented a lustful, treacherous and vindictive Pandosto living happily ever after with his family would perhaps have been harder to take than having him commit suicide. Shakespeare's solution was first to change the presentation of the king in the second part of the play. He is still presented as the penitent refusing to forget his lost queen and daughter and refusing to consider remarriage for reasons of state, but the only trace of his prototype's unnatural lust is transformed to a playful exchange when Florizel asks Leontes to speak for him for:

> . . . at your request
> My father will grant precious things as trifles.
>
> LEONTES: Would he do so, I'd beg your precious mistress,
> Which he counts but a trifle.
>
> (V.1.220 ff.)

Paulina remarks that his eye 'hath too much youth in't' and reminds him of the superior beauty of his queen, of whom he then says he thought when looking at Perdita, and so we look forward to the discovery which we know must be imminent. Shakespeare's Leontes could, of course, have been left at the end still mourning the loss of Hermione but happy in the discovery of Perdita, her marriage and his reconciliation with Polixenes. There would certainly be no reason for him to contemplate suicide. However, Shakespeare chose a more dramatic course leading to a greater measure of content. It is something which many critics suggest that Leontes has earned, but as we shall see, the ending is by no means as simple as it is sometimes made to appear, and there is certainly no direct connexion between Leontes's behaviour and the restoration of Hermione.

The impression one has when reading *Pandosto* is of a fictional world governed by Fortune. This is evident all through the story, not only in references to Fortune personified, following common Renaissance iconographic tradition, but in the very language used to tell the tale. Pandosto is fortunate in war, he and his queen live in 'fortunate content', when 'Fortune (willing to increase their happines) lent them a sonne'. But then 'Fortune envious of such happy successe, willing to shewe some signe of her inconstancie, turned her wheele, and darkned their bright sunne of prosperitie, with the mistie cloudes of mishap and misery' (see G. Bullough, *Narrative and Dramatic Sources of Shakespeare*, vol. 8, p. 157). It is Fortune who 'although blind, yet by chaunce favoring this just cause sent them within six dayes a good gale of wind' (p. 162) when Egistus is trying to escape from Pandosto. Bellaria is thought to be 'crossed with adverse Fortune' (p. 164), and complains at length of the afflictions of Fortune when imprisoned. Her new-born child seems to Pandosto to have come by Fortune, and therefore in setting her adrift in a boat he considers that he has committed her to the 'charge of Fortune' (p. 166), while her mother sees her as 'spighted by Fortune'. When the child is cast up on the shore of Sicily, Greene writes: 'Fortune minding to be wanton, willing to shewe that as she hath wrincles on her browes, so she hath dimples in her cheekes, thought after so many sower lookes, to lend a fayned smile, and after a puffing storme, to bring a pretty calme: shee began thus to dally. It fortuned a poore . . . Sheepheard . . . wandered downe toward the Sea . . .' (p. 173). Of course the love between Fawnia and Dorastus is also directed by Fortune, as is the wind which speeds their ship from Sicily.

The density and nature of the references are fairly obvious from this. Shakespeare gives a very different impression. It is not simply that in a play there is no narrator to discourse upon the nature of fortune at every turn in the action. The number of events depending simply upon chance and accident are reduced, though of course they do exist. For example, the jealousy of Leontes has something in common with the kind of violent and unexplained passion which can seize figures of romance, and which, because it seems to arise from an arbitrary stroke of fortune, can often be shed at the end without permanently tainting the man it has afflicted: one might compare the tyranny of Duke Frederick in *As You Like It*. Yet even here there is a perfunctory motivation in Leontes's misunderstanding of what he sees, and perhaps also an attempt to suggest that the audience might understand his fears in the light of traditional stories of one good and faithful friend stealing another's lady. Storms of course do just spring up, and it is chance that Antigonus happens to encounter the bear, though there is some explanation even for this accident (see below).

What there certainly is not, however, is any attempt to replace Greene's Fortune with divine or providential direction; rather, events are more often presented quite simply as consequent upon human decisions and actions. When Camillo warns Polixenes, the ships are already prepared, Camillo has the keys of the posterns and they 'take the urgent hour' (I.2.465): they do not have to wait until Fortune sends a wind. Leontes, like Pandosto, may see his child as having come to him by 'strange fortune' and entrust her future to chance, but what happens to her depends very much upon the intervention of Antigonus and his willingness to 'pawn the little blood which [he has] left/To save the innocent' (II.3.165–6) from the fire. Perdita is taken to Bohemia, she does not drift there. Indeed, rather than feeling that chance or fortune are involved here, an audience may perhaps even have a sense of the providential about this. The mariner suggests that the storm which eventually destroys him and his companions is a sign of the heavens' anger at what they are doing and Antigonus replies 'Their sacred wills be done!' (III.3.7). Later he says that he feels 'accursed' to have sworn to do it and within a few lines is eaten by a bear. His account of his vision or dream contributes to the sense we have here of some sort of superhuman guidance. We discover, in due course, that bringing Perdita to Bohemia enables the oracle of Apollo to be fulfilled. Yet, as we have seen, whatever impression we get at the time, Antigonus's dream is misleading, and we may reflect that there is nothing to suggest that the mariner's fears of heaven's disapproval exist anywhere but in his conscience. Even the bear, like the lost sheep which bring the shepherd searching along the shore to find the baby, has been startled by the hunt, a naturalistically explicable event only to be found in Shakespeare and not in Greene. Shakespeare is careful to allow the impressions to have their effect, but is equally careful, I think, to avoid providing any support for seeing the play as directed by any providential schema. Florizel blesses the time his falcon flew across Perdita's father's ground (IV.4.14–16), but he says nothing of fortune here, where he might well have done, even casually. Perdita is afraid that Polixenes may come upon them by accident: in fact he goes to the feast by design, acting upon intelligence. When they are discovered, Florizel certainly does not see himself as Fortune's fool, but is prepared to battle it out: 'Let myself and fortune/Tug for the time to come.' (IV.4.493–4). Neither is he put out when he discovers that his father has followed them to Sicilia, denying that their love would be affected even if he were accompanied by a physical manifestation of their ill fortune:

> . . . Though Fortune, visible an enemy,
> Should chase us, with my father, power no jot
> Hath she to change our loves.
>
> (V.1.215–17)

It is Camillo who suggests that the lovers should take refuge with Leontes, partly for his own purposes. They are not driven there by storms on their way to Italy. And it is Camillo who reveals the lovers' whereabouts to Polixenes, whereas Egistus hears it 'from Merchauntes of Bohemia'.

In the chapter on the structure of the play I observed that while theorists of tragicomedy expected a play to surprise the audience with its apparent wonders, these were supposed to be provided with some kind of plausible explanation. We concentrated on the one which is provided for the apparently miraculous restoration of Hermione (p. 13 ff.). The account given here of one of Shakespeare's alterations to *Pandosto* reveals a similar tendency in operation throughout the play. However extraordinary things seem, and Shakespeare often makes them seem even more incredible than they are in his source, most of them have an explanation, and sometimes a very down-to-earth explanation.

Pastoral and Romance

The lost child of royal, aristocratic or wealthy parentage saved from death, brought up by strangers as their own child and eventually discovered only when grown up, is in itself a very old narrative motif going back to Greek and Latin comedy and romance, and beyond. Such stories might involve a love affair which apparently cannot end happily, often between persons of different rank and fortune, but which comes right when the true identity of one or even both of the lovers is discovered. They frequently found expression in the pastoral mode. This is how Greene treats the subject. Shakespeare would have realized at once that *Pandosto* contained ideal material for developing into the kind of pastoral tragicomedy which was then so much in vogue throughout Europe following the enormous popularity of Guarini's *Il Pastor Fido* (see above, p. 7 ff.), and furthermore that the material had an excellent formal pedigree in comic tradition. However, it was an opportunity of which he did not choose to avail himself fully. There can be no doubt that he was well versed in the interdependent traditions of pastoral and romance and absorbed much from them which had a profound effect upon his technique as a dramatist. Yet never at any point in his career did he write anything which may be described as a simple, straightforward pastoral. What follows is an attempt to provide only a very brief account of the history and development of the pastoral and romance traditions simply in order to place Shakespeare and *The Winter's Tale*, which is often described as pastoral or romance, in relation to these traditions.

From the earliest times pastoral seems to have been a sophisticated literary mode. In the third century BC Theocritus wrote his *Idylls* about Sicilian shepherds and their songs of love. His most important Latin imitator was Virgil (1 BC), whose *Eclogues* were often taken as models in the Renaissance. In England Spenser modelled his *Shepheardes Calender* (1579) on the tradition and its influence spread widely. Quite early in its history, pastoral had been merged with romance in what became one of the most influential of all the Greek romances so popular during the Renaissance, Longus's *Daphnis and Chloe* (2–3 AD). Indeed with this work it may be said that pastoral romance originated. It was Longus who first gave the narrative a completely pastoral setting and understood the potential of a plot linking town and country, and the lives of rich and poor. In *Daphnis and Chloe* Lamon the shepherd discovers a baby boy being suckled by one of his goats and two years later his neighbour Dryas finds a baby girl suckled by one of his ewes; both children grow up together and fall in love, and at the end of the story are discovered, by the tokens left with them when they were exposed, to be the children not of poor country folk but of wealthy parents.

The convention was that pastoral was concerned with the lives of shepherds, but these, of course, are literary shepherds only distantly and tenuously related to those flute-playing rustic poets who, we are told, could be found inhabiting the mountains in Greece and Albania. The world of pastoral tradition is certainly not normally naturalistic. The shepherds' life is usually viewed with nostalgia, as an ideal which can reflect an image of lost innocence, of a golden or pre-lapsarian world. It is often contrasted with the pretensions and corruption of the contemporary court and city, and sometimes with real country life. More often than not the mood became reflective and then critical, and works included comic ridicule and satire, sometimes aimed at quite specific targets. The end was moral. George Puttenham put it very well in his account of the pastoral eclogue in his celebrated analysis of the *Arte of English Poesie* (1589). Pastoral, he wrote, was not written

> ... of purpose to counterfait or represent the rusticall manner of loves and communication: but under the vaile of homely persons, and in rude speeches to insinuate and glaunce at greater matters, and such as perchance had not bene safe to have beene disclosed in any other sort ... These Eglogues ... containe and enforme morall discipline, for the amendment of mans behaviour ...
>
> (Book I, xviii)

By the end of the sixteenth and the beginning of the seventeenth century in England the influence of the tradition was widespread. There are dialogues, debates, elegies, poems about love and religious satire all informed by it. There are, however, only a few purely pastoral plays and these tend to exploit the romantic rather than the satiric possibilities of the tradition. These were and remain anomalies, a part neither then nor since of any native dramatic tradition.

Pastoral was often combined, as we have seen, with romance. Like most terms of the sort, this is very difficult to define with any precision and can be misleading. It is a topic which has already been touched on in the first chapter when considering dramatic structures. There Shakespeare's predilection for the romantic was contrasted with Jonson's insistence on what he understood to be the classical view of comedy. However, to many of their contemporaries the distinction would not have been easy to recognize, for the kind of story outlined at the beginning of this section, which sounds like the archetypal forebear of many an Elizabethan or Jacobean romantic narrative, would also serve as an account of the plot of many a classical comedy. There was of course a difference. Writers of romantic comedies were inclined to treat their material in a way which tended to emphasize an engaging, delightful, sentimental and marvellous story, rather than the more classical ingeniously argued and skilfully manipulated plot. At its best, though, the combination of romance material with the skill in plotting and the management of intrigue to be found in classical comedy developed into a new, more shapely, vigorous and often exciting kind of vernacular comedy. The roots of the romance material on which writers drew were wide-reaching and deep. They reached into Greek romance where, as we have already seen in *Daphnis and Chloe*, they found pastoral too. They reached into the works of the European descendants of the writers of Greek romance; and also into a vernacular medieval past, much of which remained unchanged in Shakespeare's time. Here were romances and plays which contained the kind of material to which Shakespeare, and indeed others, returned again and again throughout their careers, their sophistication being measured by the transformations they wrought rather than by their ignoring such stale stuff.

The student of Shakespeare is of course primarily interested in discovering what Shakespeare made of these interrelated traditions of pastoral and romance. It turns out that the romance elements, so obvious to Jonson, are obvious to most modern students of the plays too. We can easily find elements drawn from those involved episodic tales of chivalry, of courtly gallants and beautiful ladies, of improbable and fantastic adventures in extravagant settings, of heroic feats of arms, of amazing spectacles, of long wanderings and perilous journeys through wonderful lands, of the dreadful and arbitrary afflictions of fortune, of love sudden, unrequited, or enduring and put to the test, of lovers divided and reunited, of ladies following their lovers in male disguise, of women persecuted and falsely accused, of friendships kept and broken, of parents and children lost and found and so on. For example, many of these elements are clearly apparent in *Two Gentlemen of Verona* and in *Twelfth Night*. We can see, too, how this material can be artfully and meaningfully disposed, not with the sometimes rather intrusive and clumsy didacticism of a workaday exemplary romance, but with a subtlety and sophistication which can provide a penetrating analysis of, for example, the nature and ideals of love and friendship, family relationships, or the exercise of power.

However, Shakespeare's plays, even those which have shepherds in them, can hardly ever be described strictly speaking as pastoral, unlike some of their sources. It has been pointed out that even in Greene's

Pandosto, the elements of Renaissance pastoral may be prominent but they are not essential (Salingar, *Shakespeare and the Traditions of Comedy*, p. 50). However, the structural pattern which involves withdrawal into the pastoral world, and the detached, reflective and even critical perspective it provided, can be paralleled in the change of location familiar in comedy. Sometimes there is an overt contrast between court and country as in *As You Like It*, incorporating a considerable amount of pastoralism. Sometimes the change of place and what happens there seems more important than the nature of the place: for example, it may be the case that everyone is revealed for what he or she is in the forest in *Two Gentlemen of Verona*, and there is a gesture to the pastoral model in a brief speech by Valentine expressing a preference for 'unfrequented woods' rather than 'flourishing peopled towns' (V.4.2–3); but the exiled denizens of the forest are robbers (not courtiers disguised as shepherds, consorting with real shepherds), and nothing is made of the setting in the development of the action. Sometimes the whole play may be said to be set in the other place, as, for instance, in *Twelfth Night*'s Illyria, but there are still no shepherds. Nor are there any in *The Tempest*, though here the relationship between what happens on the island and what has happened, and will happen, in the world beyond it, is closely linked. Even the change of place to the heath in *King Lear* has, interestingly, been seen in terms of an anti-pastoral, a reversal of the usual pastoral convention, where the weather is inclement, and the inhabitants, though disguised and displaced courtiers, are not shepherds – indeed some of them are feigned or genuine madmen. The comparison between the court and this wild country is disturbing and revealing.

The Winter's Tale might be thought to show pastoral influence in the pattern of court–country–court. When we look at this closely, however, we may observe that it, too, is a little unusual. The episodic nature of the fiction, the long time scale typical of romance, means that instead of our finding a central section in which major characters from the first act of the play go away from the court and spend time in an environment which provides them with a changed perspective on their own lives, and perhaps on that of the court from which they came, the focus has moved to the next generation. That is not, of course, to say that there is no relationship between the two worlds, but it is less direct, perhaps less pastoral than might at first have been thought.

Even in *As You Like It*, Shakespeare's most apparently pastoral play, instead of simply presenting us with an ideal picture of Arcadian life contrasting with and commenting on the life of the court, he adapted his source, Thomas Lodge's *Rosalynde*, in such a way that a whole range of pastoral conventions are wittily mocked, bringing them down to earth by setting them against the nature, concerns, language and imagery of ordinary village life, and making us acutely aware of their absurdity. Neither courtiers nor real rustics trying to be pastoral lovers, nor court, nor country life escape unscathed: Orlando is mocked; Phebe is not the disdainful beauty she pretends to be but a country woman with housewife's hands who should be glad of the love of her good countryman; and if courtiers express distaste at the real shepherd's lot, Touchstone can equally scorn their pretentiousness and delicacy. This is, then, no simple pastoral play, nor is it just that arid thing that seems to delight some commentators as an end in itself, a work which is a criticism of the kind in which it is written. Of course it often adopts a satirical approach to pastoral convention, but more tellingly it employs those conventions to mock men's foolishness and pretensions, especially in love where they frequently appear in their grossest and most ludicrous form.

W. W. Greg claimed that even in *The Winter's Tale*, despite their origins in Greene, the shepherd scenes owe 'nothing of their treatment to pastoral tradition, nothing to convention,' but rather come from 'life as it mirrored itself in the magic glass of the poet's imagination' (*Pastoral Poetry and Pastoral Drama*, p. 411). This makes one consider the treatment of the so-called pastoral elements of the play very carefully. What is taken from pastoral and is it treated in a pastoral fashion? Then in what sense can the treatment of the shepherd scenes be said to be taken from life?

First of all it may be that Longus's *Daphnis and Chloe*, which was certainly one of Greene's sources, was used directly by Shakespeare as a model for the hunt to frighten the sheep and rouse the bear. In the second place Greene and tradition may be said to have influenced Shakespeare in his comic treatment of the shepherds, though as we have already observed he changes this part of his source very considerably. Much of the imagined life, the apparent 'realism' which Greg observed in these scenes, may well not be consciously derived from the pastoral tradition, though it is interesting to read what P. Turner, the translator of the Penguin edition of *Daphnis and Chloe*, has to say about the characteristic presence and importance of 'touches of realism' there. He writes for example of the snow which Daphnis shakes from his legs and the flies which annoy Chloe when she is trying to make cheese. These are not there, he wrote, 'to reproduce real life: their function is to provide those points of contact the human mind demands before it will enter fully into a world of fantasy', and cites as comparisons the details of navigation in *Gulliver's Travels* and the Appendix on Newspeak

Grammar in *Nineteen Eighty Four*. Of course Gregg suggests that the realism in the shepherd scenes is rather more extensive.[1]

If the 'realism' Gregg observed and admired is not pastoral, it is certainly more traditional and literary and less from the 'English fields and lanes' than his rather romantic view suggests. For example the behaviour of Autolycus is like that of his namesake in Ovid (a rather literary origin for a native rogue!), who can '. . . eyes so bleere,/As for to make ye black things whyght and whyght things black appeere, (XI.306–7). When he announces to the audience how he will behave before stealing from the Clown, we recognize the Vice from the Morality plays as the dramatic model. The source for his trickery is, at least in part, from some of Greene's other work. In Greene's 'conny-catching' pamphlets (1592) we find accounts of sheet stealing, an explanation of the term 'snappings' to describe stolen pieces of linen (see *The Winter's Tale* IV.3.26), the trick of pretending to collapse so that there is the opportunity to take a purse from a man who goes to the thief's aid, which Shakespeare develops into a parody of the story of the Good Samaritan when Autolycus first meets the Clown; and there is an account of how cut-purses work together with a singer and seller of ballads, which resembles the account Autolycus gives of his success at the feast (IV.4.594–614). Of course these instances are in a sense 'realistic', but Shakespeare has taken them not directly from life, not from the fields and lanes, but from popular rogue literature.

The dancing of the herdsmen who have 'made themselves all men of hair' (IV.4.324), may seem at first sight to be simply the homely foolery the old Shepherd takes it for and intends to have none of. But when Polixenes asks to see it we learn from the Servant's further commendation that some of them claim to have performed at court already. But this is not the kind of performance put on by rude mechanicals like those from *A Midsummer Night's Dream*; these seem to be fairly accomplished dancers in the guise of the woodwoses or wild men we find in pageants, masques and even romances. They perform what is called a dance of satyrs which recalls those figures with 'shaggie thighs' running, leaping and gesturing in a dance full of 'swift motion' purporting to be 'antique' in Jonson's masque, *Oberon* (1611). Nor are they out of place here, for

1. There is another interesting parallel between *The Winter's Tale* and *Daphnis and Chloe*, though a conscious connection is unlikely. Longus is a self-conscious narrator who can comment on his handling of the story with self-deprecating humour. This, P. Turner says, 'does more than anything else to assist the reader's suspension of disbelief, even when the story seems a trifle tall' (p. 12). There is a striking similarity between this observation and that of a number of critics of *The Winter's Tale* remarking on the repeated self-conscious references to the work's fictionality.

the association of satyr and pastor as supporters of the figure of Tragicomedy is there for all to see on the titlepage of Jonson's *Works* (1616), and it had, in any case, been made by Renaissance theorists who looked to the Greek satyr play as a principal authority for pastoral tragicomedy. Again something which, from a cursory examination, might well seem to be taken from life rather than from tradition turns out to have rather more complex and sophisticated associations.

Pageants and Masques

Those 'men of hair' lead us to pageant and masque. The gap of sixteen years between the two parts of the play is announced by a figure whose background seems to lie in the more popular of the two entertainments, the pageant. Personifications like this, indeed of Time himself, can be found there and that is one of the most obvious sources for the workaday style of his speech. If it is stilted, conventional and old fashioned, it may well be intended to seem to be the appropriate utterance of the traditional emblematic figure of Time, an old man with an hour glass. One may compare the use which is made of the consciously archaic speech of the narrator, Gower, in *Pericles* to frame and distance the events of that play and give it the air of the antique. The style of Time's speech underlines its function. It reflects a structure which is deliberately unclassical, and emphasizes the linear movement of the tale. That we are aware of the long-drawn-out, slow passage of time is crucial to the play, but we would not want to sit through numerous scenes which created that awareness, for to do so would certainly bore us, and our attention would wander. It is Time's function to perform that task in one speech and, as I have suggested already, to contribute to other effects which are working here.

Satyrs link the play not only with the pageant but with the masque, and they are not the only, and by no means the most important, links which have been suggested by scholars. Masques were lavish courtly entertainments, frequently devised to celebrate important events. They combined verse, music and dancing, were extravagantly costumed, with changeable perspective scenery and elaborate machinery capable of producing amazing effects. If one reads Bacon's description of a masque in his essay on 'Masques and Triumphs', it is easy to understand why critics have suggested a connection with *The Winter's Tale*. He speaks of 'fools, satyrs, baboons, wild-men, antics, beasts, sprites, witches, Ethiopes, pigmies, turquets, nymphs, rustics, Cupids, statuas moving and the like', and later asks that masque music 'be recreative and with some strange changes'. In *The Winter's Tale* we have one fool, the Clown, wild men doing a satyr's dance, one beast, rustics and finally what appears to be a statue moving, while music which might well be called 'recreative' is played. Certainly the whole final scene is stage-managed by Paulina rather as if she were a masque presenter. We also know that statues that came to life were thought some time later to be the stuff of masques, for the same device occurs in Campion's *Lord's Masque* and in Beaumont's *Masque of the Inner Temple*, which were both presented at court in 1613, and they may even have been influenced by court performances of *The Winter's Tale*. It is possible that Shakespeare's treatment of the return of Hermione might have been influenced by the spectacle and wonder and transformation scenes of masques, though he would have known, too, that Guarini's prescription for tragicomedy included the arousing of wonder in the audience, so it is hard to be sure how much responsibility we can lay at the door of those courtly entertainments.

Of course the idea of apparently bringing a statue to life, however convincing one finds the argument that the staging of the scene itself owes something to masque presentation, may well owe little or nothing to that sort of entertainment. It reminds us of the story of Pygmalion and Galatea told by Ovid in his *Metamorphoses*. Pygmalion, whose art is 'wondrous', carves the statue of a woman. The ivory from which it is made seems to be real flesh and the image appears to be alive. It is an ideal image far exceeding the beauty or grace of any of Nature's creations and better than anything of which she is capable, an example of the power of art to add to, mend, or improve on her work. Pygmalion is enamoured of his beautiful work and in answer to his prayer to Venus the statue comes to life. The Gentleman's description of the art of Julio Romano and the description of the statue itself in the final scene, especially the remarks about the statue seeming to be alive and have blood in its veins, show some close similarities to the Ovidian narrative.

Shakespeare had introduced masques into his plays before, and in *The Tempest* masques and masque devices play an important part. In *The Winter's Tale* it is much more difficult to be sure of the extent of the influence and disentangle it from what is already a skilful synthesis of a variety of materials. However, part of the effect produced by the conclusion may have some affinity with that produced by the masque. It was customary at the end of the masque for the final celebratory dance to incorporate the audience. The idea was that the harmony demonstrated in the action of the masque, the triumph of virtue over vice, reached out to include the courtly watchers, thus obliterating, as it were, the division between art and life. At the end of this play there are two audiences: a courtly audience on stage watches the apparent transformation and, when it takes place, becomes incorporated in it, and then there is the audience in the theatre. The members of this audience are aware – indeed they have been reminded of it throughout the play – that they are watching a work of fiction. They are not taken into the harmony and often do not feel in tune with it. Many seem to feel dissatisfied or uneasy because they think this is the kind of solution which is possible only in art and not in life. In life Hermione would not, indeed could not, do as she does here and remain hidden for sixteen years, and the time lost from their lives and marriage would be less easily passed over. It is a response which encourages some to try to see faults in the harmony of the reconciliation between Leontes and Hermione, and they ask, for example, why she doesn't speak to her husband. While this dissatisfaction testifies to a problem inherent in the final harmony, and one which is intended to be there, I doubt the fact that Perdita is spoken to and Leontes only embraced is significant. Indeed Hermione 'hangs about his neck' (V.3.112). Silence and gesture are better than words. If we do recall the end of the masque because of the spectacular theatrical effect and the amazement it produces, our perception of any similarity will make us all the more conscious of the striking difference. There is no pretence at providing a masque-like, harmonious conclusion for the audience. Things happen in fictions which cannot happen in life. Unlike a masque, the play does not attempt to cross the line. Once again in the play the conclusion reinforces an awareness of the difference.

I have tried to show in this chapter how Shakespeare's major source was modified and developed using other diverse material. The syntheses and transformations wrought here are never simple. An examination of them, however, may help the student both to understand something of the artist's enormous technical skill and, by noticing what he expands on, or emphasizes, and what he ignores, to understand something of his intentions.

3. Themes and Ideas in the Play

Introductory

Most critics of Shakespeare's last plays devote some time and space to the discussion of 'themes'. When comparing what they have written it is sometimes rather difficult to be sure precisely what constitutes a theme, or perhaps to tell where one ends and another begins. In theory a theme, as distinct from the plot or subject of the work, is one of those important central ideas, explicit or implicit, which may be perceived as running like a continuous thread through the work. Sometimes one theme seems to the majority of critics and audiences to be more important than any other, as for example does jealousy in *Othello*. In other works several themes may be treated, and these are accorded differing importance depending on the writer. Sometimes what is a single theme to one becomes subdivided into several by another. When plays are considered together in a group, like the last plays, it is usual for themes common to several or all of them to be identified. It would indeed be rather surprising if similar ideas were not in Shakespeare's mind over the comparatively short period in which these plays were written, especially as they are based on substantially similar source materials. As it does when making other kinds of comparisons between the plays, identifying common themes can lead to a diminution of our perception of the plays' individuality. However, a consideration of the themes identified by different critics also demonstrates very clearly that these plays certainly cannot be seen as a hermetically sealed group, for themes found in them can be found in works throughout Shakespeare's career. To name but a few topics, he had an abiding interest in love, friendship, jealousy, justice, mercy, forgiveness, reconciliation, separation, loss, reunion, relations between parents and children, nature, art, and many others. These are the basic common currency of critical discussions of all the plays.

Nature and Art

The theme which has perhaps received the most discussion over the years is the treatment of the relationship between nature and art in the play. Many critics have felt, like G. Wilson Knight in *The Crown of Life*: '"Great nature" is our over-ruling deity' (p. 90), though they have not always meant quite the same thing by it. The crucial passage in the play with which all discussions of nature and art begin is what has sometimes been called the great debate between Perdita and Polixenes in Act IV.4.71–108. To get this into proper dramatic perspective it should be noticed that this exchange occupies only a very small part of the long scene in which it is placed, certainly one disproportionate to its generally agreed importance, and takes a comparatively short time to perform. Much more space is given to Perdita's distribution of flowers, her wish for flowers of the spring and the exchange with Florizel about their mutual affection. This of course is entirely appropriate for the first part of this important scene is intended to establish Perdita's beauty, her grace and her honest relationship with Florizel. The exchange with Polixenes is a digression which interrupts the flower giving. As a dramatic technique it is masterly. An interruption always commands more attention than the space or the number of lines it takes. However, some critics have, I think, made a little too much of what is after all a reflection of an entirely familiar and conventional argument. However great the debate may have been elsewhere, what takes place here can scarcely be called a great debate. It would indeed have been something of an old chestnut to many in the audience.

The view which Perdita expresses is sometimes called primitivist, and, linked to that found in Montaigne's essay 'Of the Cannibals' translated into English by John Florio and published in 1603, which Shakespeare used when writing Gonzalo's speech on an ideal commonwealth in *The Tempest* (II.1.150). Montaigne supposed for the purpose of his argument in the essay that the New World provided an example of an environment free from the corruptions of civilization. He refers to fruits which 'our selves have altered by our artificiall devices' as 'bastardized' and says that it is these that should be called 'savage' rather than those wild fruits produced by 'nature of herselfe'. There is 'no reason, arte should gaine the point of honour of our great and puissant mother Nature'. Man's artifice has 'over-choaked hir; yet where-ever hir puritie shineth, she makes our vaine, and frivolous enterprises wonderfully ashamed'. He makes an analogy between the Indians who inhabit this New World and the uncultivated fruit, and finds both preferable to the effects of civilization and cultivation. This New World can be used as a measure of the sophisticated depravity of the Old World. It is, in a sense, the same sort of contrast familiar in the pastoral tradition, where the world of the court and the city is set beside that of an idealized countryside to the disadvantage of the former.

The weight of sophisticated contemporary intellectual opinion was, however, on Polixenes' side: some of the imperfections of fallen nature could be repaired by art, which since it was itself the product of man's intelligence and ingenuity was therefore natural. It is the kind of modish argument that one might expect to be in the mouth of a Renaissance prince fresh from court. Indeed the force of the argument draws apparent, perhaps polite, agreement from Perdita – 'So it is' (IV.4.98) – at least in theory, though it is clear that she has no intention of allowing the argument to change her practice as a gardener. Support for Polixenes' view finds a fairly definitive, if lengthy, expression in Puttenham's *Art of English Poesie* (pp. 253–7). Puttenham's argument seems particularly apposite because it draws extensively on horticultural analogies. He sees art as an 'ayde and coadiutor to nature, or peradventure a meane to supply her wants'.

It is appropriate that Perdita should take the view she does. She has been presented so far in the play as a young, sheltered innocent brought up in an uncomplicated rural society, a pastoral world, where she has as yet no experience of the frailty of a nature seriously in need of repair. Hers is a simple, unsophisticated view, which sees art as analogous to face painting to deceive men, or even as blasphemous pride in that it seems to be trying to equal the power and function of 'great creating nature'. Her view then seems both natural and appropriate to her role as the ideal heroine of pastoral. An interesting effect is produced: members of the audience who recognize the familiar argument will accept the good sense of what Polixenes says. He has won the argument. However, Perdita's words reinforce the picture of her which has already been established, and critics and audiences alike are rather drawn to her. The Arden editor is a case in point: 'The argument does her no less honour than it does Polixenes, though, *qua* argument, he has the better of it' (note on the Arden edition IV.4.88–97).

This exchange relates to the rest of the play in two ways. Most obviously and immediately the audience is aware of a certain dramatic irony. If one interprets the horticultural analogy on grafting in terms of human relationships, then Polixenes seems to be recommending a union of the kind he is shortly to condemn. The same analogy can be used to illustrate several arguments. Perhaps what is really being demonstrated here in the most unobtrusive of ways is one of the most familiar topics in the play. We are constantly being reminded that what we are watching is a fiction and we are asked to give credence to it as a fiction. That does not mean we treat it as trivial and of no significance, but it means that we do not treat it as being like life. Polixenes speaks about art and nature, not about marriages between princes and commoners. The events, and the irony they produce remind us that there is a world of difference between artistic theory and life.

Modern audiences are sometimes disturbed not just by Polixenes' apparently total *volte face* when faced with a practical opportunity of demonstrating his theory by welcoming the union of Perdita with the young prince but, granting that art and marriage are two very different things, are also disturbed at his lack of egalitarianism. Perdita's behaviour may 'smack of something . . . Too noble for this place' (IV.4.158 ff), but to him she is still only a 'knack . . . worthy a herdsman' (425–32). While a seventeenth-century audience no doubt would have wanted the lovers to win through just as much as we do, they would have been less surprised and outraged by the king's attitude than audiences sometimes are today. It would have been what was expected of the Renaissance prince concerned for his line and the well-being of his kingdom. All audiences know that Perdita will prove royal and will consequently satisfy Polixenes' view about marriage, and amusingly also her own more naïve view about the unnaturalness of grafting and inter-breeding.

In Renaissance literature virtue was frequently reflected in noble birth. The nature of the relationship between noble birth and noble behaviour in real life was a much debated question. To characters in the play Perdita seems to provide support for the opinion that true nobility should be judged by behaviour, manners and merit rather than by descent, a view which had already been developed particularly in the writing of some Italian theorists. There was, of course, no question that noble birth did not ensure noble deeds, many Renaissance villains provide testimony to that, as does the Leontes of the first part of the play. Upbringing, circumstances and the vagaries of human nature accounted for lapses in noble behaviour and those who failed to live up to their birth bore a heavier responsibility for their misdeeds than those whose birth led to lower expectations. The question of the parts played by nature and nurture was still a live one, and is important both in Spenser's *Faerie Queene* and in *The Tempest*. Perdita's noble behaviour turns out to accord with her birth: nobility shines through her rustic nurture. If this seems to be a disappointingly easy solution to the modern audience, to a seventeenth-century audience it would have been the expected and acceptable conclusion of romance.

The exchange about nature and art also looks forward to the conclusion of the play. What appears to be happening at first is that the skill of Julio Romano has produced a statue which is so like life that it seems only to lack breath. His skill would, remarks the Third Gentleman, 'beguile Nature of her custom' (V.2.97) could he have given that, and had he eternal life, like nature. The lifelike nature of the statue is dilated upon at some length in the final scene. One thing that strikes Leontes is that the statue is more wrinkled than Hermione was and Paulina observes that this is a sign of the carver's excellence, making her 'As she lived now' (V.3.32). These descriptions recall another passage in Puttenham which praises the poet or maker for work which 'issues from an excellent sharp and quick invention, holpen by a cleare and bright phantasie and imagination'. Such work is not a naturalistic copy of an original like that which he says painters produce, nor the kind of thing which the gardener produces when he helps nature grow finer flowers, nor like the product of the carpenter who uses natural wood to make something which has no original in nature. Instead the artist is working 'even as nature herselfe . . . by her owne peculiar vertue and proper instinct and not by example' and is most admired when 'most naturall and least artificiall'. Julio Romano is not just copying nature, but imagining a real woman sixteen years older and convincing us that that is what she would be like now: giving her as it were a continuing life in the artist's imagination rather than in the real world.

When we find that the reason for all this admiration is that the statue is not an excellent example of Julio Romano's art but nature's work, the real Hermione, it is sometimes said to be a demonstration of the superiority of nature to art and presumably a final voice in favour of Perdita's argument, or at the least that 'Nature transcends Art when the statue of Hermione moves' (Frank Kermode, *The Tempest*, Arden, p. xxxxv). Yet if these scenes have demonstrated anything, they have shown how people are prepared to accept that art can be so like life, that one can take life for art. Pliny tells a famous story of how a painting of grapes by Zeuxis was pecked by birds. It is the reverse which happens here. The courtiers think that the real Hermione is a wonderful, lifelike statue. There can be no doubt that Leontes prefers the real Hermione to a statue, the real woman to a work of art. That should hardly surprise us: under such circumstances we should all prefer nature to art. But notice that there is no choice between the two here. There is no statue, only Hermione. The comparison is made by courtiers who think that they are comparing a statue with a woman, but are in fact praising a woman for being like a woman. One can hardly say that nature is here proved to be superior to art, when it turns out that only nature is present and the yardstick for praising art was naturalness. There is not a contest. On reflection surely one is struck, as before, by the ease with which the two can be confused. If the exchange between Perdita and Polixenes was about the naturalness of art, this scene, while at first seeming to demonstrate the same idea, actually demonstrates the artfulness of nature.

When we watch mother and daughter standing side by side, both beautiful, the one mature and the other young, and see in them an image of the continuance of nature, it is tempting to accept Kermode's borrowing from Yeats's poem 'Sailing to Byzantium' to describe the experience: 'Whatever is begotten, born and dies' is nobler than 'monuments of unageing intellect' (*Signet*, p. xxxv). Yet just as shepherdesses only turn out to be princesses in works of fiction, so it is surely only by the art of the dramatist that a queen, presumed dead, can be concealed for sixteen years and then return. As the stress on the fictionality of what we have been experiencing throughout the play reminds us, this kind of thing only happens in art. It is not a question simply of accepting one argument or the other, or preferring nature to art or considering it nobler, or vice versa; it is rather a question of understanding the nature of the arguments, of considering the relationship between art and nature, and appreciating the function of art. It sharpens one's awareness of the gap between the real and the ideal, and makes one acutely aware both of human shortcomings and human aspirations.

Grace

Considerable attention has also been given to references to grace in the play. As one might expect these are usually of most interest to allegorists, especially Christian ones. When one looks closely at the examples in the play, however, it must be said that one finds some difficulty in tracing a single coherent theme.

Commentators often begin by trying to give special significance to Hermione's use of the word in a playful exchange with Leontes in Act I:

> My last good deed was to entreat his stay.
> What was my first? It has an elder sister,
> Or I mistake you. O, would her name were Grace!
> (I.2.97–9)

or her observation when dispatched to prison by Leontes: 'This action I now go on/Is for my better grace' (II.1.121–2). What this means is not quite clear, though most of the problem seems to come from the metaphor behind the word 'action'. Is it legal, meaning something like indictment; theatrical, meaning the part Hermione has to play; or military, suggesting a fight to defend her honour? None of them fits very well. 'For [her] better grace' seems to mean that going to prison is to her credit, increases rather than decreases her honour. Perhaps behind it lies the familiar idea that affliction tests and improves one. Dion's last words in the scene in which he and Cleomenes visit the oracle of Apollo (III.1.22) are: 'gracious be the issue'. S. L. Bethell remarks that this 'reminds us of the repeated references to grace in previous scenes' and concludes that 'at the end of this present scene grace can be taken only in its full theological sense, as a power for good infused by God into the soul' (p. 85). This seems to be reading rather a lot into the remark which may well be no more than the expression of a wish that the outcome prove to be 'happy' or 'fortunate'. Perdita is described by Time as having 'grown in grace/Equal with wond'ring', which probably means that men's wonder has kept pace with the growth of her grace or that it has grown so much that it makes men wonder at it. It has been suggested that the adult Perdita in Act IV stands for grace and nature, and Hermione too has been described in terms of natural grace.

Theologically speaking grace is the supernatural aid of God given to man to assist in his sanctification. No theologian has ever doubted the need for it but there has always been disagreement about the way it is bestowed. The orthodox view of the medieval Church was that man in his natural fallen state deserved damnation but that sufficient grace was available to all and would increase and lead to salvation if man co-operated. The reformers, while holding differing views, generally tended to take a more rigid and limited view of the availability of grace. One can see how Leontes's life might remind a Christian allegorist of a pattern of sin, repentance ('A saint-like sorrow') and redemption. The restoration of Hermione does not depend upon Leontes's penitence. He himself stresses that he cannot forget his evil or forgive himself, whatever Cleomenes claims that the heavens have dine. Hermione's return might then be seen as an act of grace, something strictly undeserved but which Leontes's condition shows that he is prepared for and can make something of. However, despite the fact that Shakespeare, as has often been observed, tends to reduce the influence of fortune usual in romance, he does not anywhere seriously suggest (as Bethell proposes, p. 102) that it is providence that controls events instead. Some consider more cautiously that while Shakespeare is not overtly writing about grace or any other theological matter the pattern of events may remind an audience of similar patterns in Christian doctrine and in this way affect its understanding of the work, operating as it were analogously, or figuratively. For example, one might consider that the return of Hermione is *like* an act of grace, rather than actually going as far as suggesting that it *is* an example of grace, or further, and seeing it as a demonstration of the theological doctrine. In the same way, one's response to the loss of innocence at the opening of the play may be affected by thinking of it as being like the fall: a 'Paradise . . . lost . . . through . . . insane delusion' as Schanzer describes it (*Review of English Literature*, p. 22). How far such patterns were consciously in Shakespeare's mind of course one cannot tell, for until quite recently they would have been familiar to the whole population.

Northrop Frye extends this approach with considerable subtlety, arguing that Hermione is to be associated with a grace which is not 'Christian or theological' and not therefore 'superior to the order of nature, but a secular analogy of Christian grace . . . identical with nature' ('Recognition in *The Winter's Tale*'). He suggests that it is similar to the grace Spenser celebrates in *The Faerie Queene* Book VI. Certainly by Book VI Spenser was not primarily concerned with matters theological, but with that grace which animates the social behaviour of the courteous man and woman. As Calidore learns from Colin Clout, when he sees the vision of the Graces dancing on Mount Acidale, their gifts are granted only to those 'whom they of them selves list so to grace' (VI.x.20). Courtesy is not learned, nor are the gifts of the Graces earned or achieved by man's efforts or earnest desire. The analogy with Christian grace is obvious. For Spenser grace made manifest in courtly courtesy was, as one of the speakers in Castiglione's *The Courtier* observed, the 'gift of nature and the heavens'. But neither in Spenser's Book VI, nor in Frye's view of *The Winter's Tale* is the grace in question the equivalent of theological grace. For Frye, the return of Hermione, this act of secular grace, leads us back to a 'real world' not on to a spiritual one, yet it is a world 'without the customary qualities of reality. It is the world symbolized by nature's power of renewal; it is the world we want; it is the world we hope our gods would want for us if they were worth worshipping' (*A Natural Perspective*, 1965, p. 116).

The way in which this 'beautiful gift' (which is the meaning of the name Calidore, the hero of Spenser's book) is shown in human behaviour is the subject of a series of episodes in *The Faerie Queene*. It is manifest not only in the actions of the characters, but in what Castiglione referred to as a 'certain grace', an immediately attractive manner and demeanour. Perdita and Spenser's Pastorella both seem to be possessed of this, and both of them are presented as earthly beings reflecting higher qualities. Perdita's reputation, which far exceeds what one would normally expect to find in such a lowly place, has reached the court: Camillo speaks of her as of 'rare note' (IV.2.42). Florizel describes the sheep-shearing feast as 'a meeting of the petty gods, And [Perdita] the queen on't'. (IV.4.4–5), and later praises her perfections:

> What you do
> Still betters what is done . . .
> Each your doing,
> So singular in each particular,
> Crowns what you are doing in the present deeds,
> That all your acts are queens.
>
> (IV.4.136–46)

Even Polixenes remarks that

> nothing she does or seems
> But smacks of something greater than herself,
> Too noble for this place.
>
> (IV.4.157–9)

while the Gentleman who brings the court news of Perdita's and Florizel's arrival in Sicilia describes Perdita as

> a creature,
> Would she begin a sect, might quench the zeal
> Of all professors else, make proselytes
> Of who she but bid follow . . .
> Women will love her that she is a woman
> More worth than any man; men that she is
> The rarest of all women.
>
> (V.1.106–12)

Pastorella, in *The Faerie Queene*, is, for comparison, like

> . . . some miracle of heavenly hew
> . . . downe to them descended in that earthly vew.
>
> And soothly sure she was full fayre of face,
> And perfectly well shapt in every lim,
> Which she did more augment with modest grace,
> And comely carriage of her count'nance trim,
> That all the rest like lesser lamps did dim:
> Who her admiring as some heavenly wight,
> Did for their soveraine godesse her esteeme,
> And caroling her name both day and night,
> The fayrest *Pastorella* her by name did hight.
>
> (VI.ix.8 and 9)

Thinking about the treatment of grace in Spenser and Shakespeare in these ways undoubtedly enhances one's understanding of aspects of the text, but there are very clear limits on what can be made of grace as a theme in the play.

Time

Time has also been identified as an important theme in the play. The figure of Time acting as a kind of chorus, the 'wide gap of time' dividing the two parts of the play, the contrast between the generations, the cycle of the seasons, and the contrast between new life, death and regeneration seem to point to its significance. It is a theme which appears in different ways in all the last plays. The long, slow passage of time is most obvious in *Pericles*. In *The Tempest*, in which the stage time and the time taken in the fiction are closely related, timing is crucial, as Frye observes: 'Like all magicians [Prospero] observes time closely ("The very minute bids thee ope thine ear," he says to Miranda), and his charms are effective only if he follows the rhythm of time . . . This feeling of time ramifies into all the imagery of *The Tempest*' (*A Natural Perspective*, 1965, pp. 152–3). One is also very conscious in *The Tempest* of the relationship between the present taking place on the stage, and the past, for the events one witnesses have developed from crimes, injustices and faults long ago. The whirligig of time has indeed brought 'in his revenges', but wisdom averts a revenge tragedy and, as in *The Winter's Tale*, the loving union between members of a younger generation newly grown to adulthood promises a better future. However, like the theme of grace in the play, one should be cautious not to exaggerate and seek to make much of trifles. For example, there is an obvious narrative reason for the nine months Polixenes has spent at the court of Leontes; and the time gap between the play's two parts – about which Shakespeare is not quite so consistently precise as some critics suggest – is more or less the minimum in which Perdita could grow up and become the object of Florizel's affections. While whatever we think about Leontes's deserving, or earning, the return of Hermione by his penitent suffering, time is certainly needed for the change he undergoes to be presented with plausibility.

Greene's *Pandosto* had the rather portentous subtitle 'The Triumph of Time', but it was a commonplace, a proverbial saying popular with Greene as with others, and means very little more there than that in the end all is revealed and Truth, Time's daughter (as another familiar saying has it: *veritas filia temporis*), is delivered. One may then ask what special meaning the theme of time has in Shakespeare's play. Shakespeare's personification of Time seems only a pale and shabby cipher for the traditionally powerful and ambiguous iconographic figure, the destroyer of all things – *edax rerum* – and the father of Truth. Instead he is a pasteboard pageant figure with his limping verse cobbling together the tragic and comic parts of the play. One thing it certainly does is contribute to the much commented on fictionality of the work. It would indeed be hard to forget that one was watching a play, for there is no attempt to conceal the time gap: quite the contrary, a personification addresses the audience directly and even somewhat ineptly, presenting himself as the teller of the tale who can 'slide/O'er sixteen years' (IV.1.5–6), having no respect for neo-classical rules about the unity of time, or place for that matter. He reminds the audience that should it consider the events he presents to be stale compared with the 'glistening of this present', 'the freshest things now reigning' will become stale in their turn. Clumsy his verse may be but what he says reminds the audience of something serious. The perspectives of time and art change, and paradoxically the feeling that one enjoys a more sophisticated perception of the world than that presented in the play one is viewing may make one all the more acutely aware of the transience of what one values so highly in the present, for as this is to us, so we will be to others. The formula is familiar and perhaps most striking when it appears as a *memento mori*, as the utterance of a skeletal figure from the grave, warning 'as I am now, so you will be'. Throughout the play this double sense of fictionality, of unreality is balanced against an awareness of the relevance of the artifice to the life and world of the contemporary audience.

It is to argue perhaps a little too inventively to see here, as Inga-Stina Ewbank has suggested, 'a vehicle for the exploration of the meanings of time – in the sense of what time does to man'. Her view emphasizes more than that of most critics the existence of time as a 'controlling and shaping figure behind the dramatic structure and technique' of the play (in *Casebook*, p. 99). However, we are aware throughout of the presentation of different views of time: the essentially linear, dealing with time as change, both bringing decay and revealing hidden truth; and the cyclic, which at its simplest appears in seasonal change. In a sense, when Hermione and Perdita are restored to Leontes his dark winter is over and a new spring begins. It is the kind of second chance one finds only in fiction, yet even here the clock cannot be put back, sixteen years have passed, and Hermione's wrinkles are real. It reminds us that whatever the art of the dramatist can do, we still have to face the reality of the changes time makes.

Forgiveness and Restoration

A number of themes which may be grouped together as essentially similar are those which have to do with reconciliation, mercy, forgiveness, restoration and regeneration. These are related to others already discussed here and elsewhere, and may also be traced in different ways in other plays, particularly in the other last plays. In *Pericles* only restoration is prominent, for though there is a reunion of a father with a mother and daughter he thought dead, since the separation was not brought about by the father's faults there is no need for forgiveness. In *Cymbeline* sons are separated from their father, a daughter flees to meet a lover she has married against her father's wishes, and a wife is misjudged and her life threatened. Here restoration, reconciliation and forgiveness are all needed at the conclusion of the play. In *The Tempest* Prospero's own fault was committed years before, as were the far greater crimes of his enemies, and the emphasis moves to mercy and forgiveness. In *The Winter's Tale* all of them are present. These themes have been called life-affirming in contrast to those life-denying ones found at the beginning of the play. Sometimes one feels that critics give a too enthusiastic account of the regeneration and new life and that the memory of sin and loss has been too easily forgotten, with the conclusion treated rather sentimentally. More recently one has sometimes encountered exactly the opposite reaction: some critics seem rather too ready to find any suggestion of a harmonious conclusion false and insincere. Often, as the brief account of critical views of the play to be found in this book indicates, the themes have been seen as paralleling Christian experience, and many link forgiveness and restoration with a consideration of grace in the play. According to some there is an explicit reference 'to the symbolism of the Christian faith, in which Christ is said to have ransomed the world, though this world must be destroyed by fire so that the new Jerusalem may arise from its ashes, an eternal city' (Bethell, p. 102). This is an extreme view, and many interpreters simply point out that ideas like those to do with mercy and forgiveness, especially when associated with justice and injustice (as they are here and elsewhere amongst Shakespeare's plays, in *Measure for Measure* for example), were – and indeed still are – important both in personal relations and in maintaining the fabric of ordinary civilized social life.

Parents and Children

A theme which is often identified as shared between all the last plays is the relationship between the generations. In *Cymbeline*, *Pericles*, *The Winter's Tale* and *The Tempest* the dramatic impact of the young men is, for the most part, subsidiary. The young women are much more prominent and it is they who are instrumental in restoring the lives of the older generation, sometimes directly and actively as in *Pericles*, and sometimes, as in *The Winter's Tale* and *The Tempest*, playing a more passive but equally important and significant role. Perdita's return to Sicilia precipitates the events which bring about the conclusion of the play, but she has no inkling of what will ensue. Miranda's love for Ferdinand, while genuine, is the consequence of her father's management, and is part of his reconciliation with Alonso. The perspective which these young women's innocence provides is refreshing in contrast with the calculating cynicism of some of those who are more experienced, and their purity is impressive. However, they are often in need of wisdom. Without Prospero's powers of discrimination all men seem marvels to Miranda; and while we may find the arguments of Perdita in Act IV appealing, we know full well that the weight of intellectual support is behind those of Polixenes.

Many treatments of the relationship between parents and children tend to present the parents in their declining years, and it is worth pausing to remark that there is little evidence to support this. They may well be worn down with care and loss, and as a consequence might seem, at times, to be prematurely aged, but they are not decrepit, as even a cursory examination of the text will indicate. It would be ludicrous to try to calculate their ages as if they were real people, for as we know Shakespeare did not feel compelled to be consistent in this way. Yet Pericles, after all his trials, feels able to make for Tharsus to 'strike' Cleon, had he not been diverted to Ephesus by Diana. Prospero is simply too energetic to be taken for a geriatric during the play. Miranda was three years old when they came to the island twelve years before, and he speaks of her as a third of his life when he gives her in marriage to Ferdinand, which may mean that he has spent a third of his life bringing her up. His intention to 'retire' to his dukedom in Milan and there devote every 'third thought' to his 'grave' has been not unnaturally taken to mean that he envisages his life as moving towards its end, but it is difficult to see why Shakespeare should particularly want us to think about him as being old here. Perhaps 'retire' simply means 'go back', and when at Milan he will follow the injunction given to all Christian princes, and indeed to all men, to regard their end. If one were to calculate the age of Leontes and Hermione from 'evidence' in the play, then one would conclude that they are very probably both in their forties. In other words all these characters are if not young, certainly not old, and there is some point of speaking about a regeneration and new life for them as well as for the children. If this were not so, the restoration brought about by the children, so often remarked on by critics, would be rather hollow.

Generally the relationship between children and parents cannot be portrayed as one of close family affection, for, with the exception of Miranda, they are shown as separated. Indeed the hardships they suffer are often directly or indirectly attributable to parental failings. In *Cymbeline* and in *Pericles* the younger generation endures hardship in adult life; in *The Winter's Tale* and *The Tempest* both Perdita and Miranda suffer as children, and Perdita seems destined to do so again as an adult when threatened by Polixenes, but all triumph over their afflictions and their final restoration is all the more affecting because of their resolute endurance. In them seems to be the promise of better things, of fresh beginnings.

The Faithful Woman

If the young women in these plays are marked by courage and steadfast endurance in the face of adversity, Hermione also shares these characteristics. Just as children exposed, lost and then found is a common narrative motif, so she too belongs to a traditional type: the calumniated woman who remains faithful and constant. Shakespeare developed this motif in each of the last plays, with the exception of *The Tempest*. There is a great deal in *Cymbeline* and *The Winter's Tale* about trust and lack of trust, especially between the sexes. Nor is it simple: Cymbeline trusted his queen, Posthumus did not trust Imogen, nor Leontes Hermione, and all of them suffered the consequences. Naïve and undiscriminating trust is as dangerous as jumping too hastily to conclusions and failing to recognize, and have faith in, true virtue. Claudio in *Much Ado About Nothing* is an earlier prototype of this fallible male. Posthumus was at least duped by Iachimo, Leontes entirely self-deceived apparently by the show of affection a man might expect his wife to show to his dear boyhood friend. Both men move from a seemingly complete trust of one woman to a condemnation of the infidelity and sexual proclivities of women in general.

Of course the women prove not only trustworthy but enduringly faithful. Imogen's role in *Cymbeline* is to demonstrate her qualities actively, like an earlier heroine, Julia, in *The Two Gentlemen of Verona*, and in true romance tradition she is prepared to brave the wilds in male disguise in search of Posthumus. Hermione's role is to wait patiently for many years for the return of her daughter, which seems unlikely and is certainly not unambiguously promised by the oracle. In *The Winter's Tale*, if one adds to Hermione and Perdita the fearless virtue, the loyalty and the fidelity of Paulina over the long bleak years of her mistress's concealment, one might be able to identify a theme in this play, clearly echoed elsewhere in the last plays, demonstrating female virtue and fortitude. A clear eye may discern here a powerful force for good, very different from those sentimental heroines of Victorian criticism.

Jealousy and Friendship

Among many other themes identified but less often developed in any detail, perhaps because their treatment in the play is less extended, one often finds jealousy. Here it is a powerful sudden affliction which destroys the harmony of the Sicilian court. Unlike Greene, Shakespeare does not seek to give Leontes any basis for his jealousy at all: in *Pandosto* Bellaria often went into Egistus's bedchamber to see that all was well. Whatever pains some producers and critics take to give psychological plausibility to the events in the second scene of the first act, Shakespeare seems to give it little attention. Leontes's love for Hermione turns swiftly to hatred and he seems to be imprisoned alone in a mad private world, separated from his true self, the just king, loving husband and father, and true friend he has been known to be.

Though Shakespeare not infrequently treats this subject in the last plays, the character most frequently cited for comparison here is, naturally enough, Othello; although, beyond the fact that both plays treat of jealousy, similarities are not really very close. A. C. Bradley, in a famous lecture on *Othello*, drew a distinction between the complexity of Othello's passion and the simple 'feelings of jealousy proper' experienced by Leontes, 'the essentially jealous man', one who experiences the intolerable 'thought of another man's possessing the woman he loves . . . the sense of insult and the impulse of revenge . . . at times most violent' (*Shakespearean Tragedy*, p. 194). To begin with, *Othello* is very much concerned with the way in which Othello is made jealous and the consuming growth of his passion. No Iago is instrumental in deceiving Leontes: his deception springs entirely from within himself. One of the ways in which Iago was able to arouse his general's suspicions was by asking if Cassio had gone wooing with Othello; and indeed he proved often to have done one of the services which faithful friends traditionally performed – sometimes with disastrous consequences – which was to have gone between Othello and Desdemona as an intermediary. It was a common literary topic that the friend faithful in all else, so similar to his companion in virtue and in taste that he was often called another self, should fall in love with his friend's lady, and perhaps even succeed in stealing her. As Robert Burton, the author of the *Anatomy of Melancholy*, wrote: the jealousy of love

> . . . will make the nearest and dearest friends fall out; they will endure all other things to be common, goods, lands, moneys, participate of each [other's] pleasures, and take in good part any disgrace, injuries in another kind; but . . . in this they will suffer nothing, have no co-rivals.
>
> (Part III, Sec. iii, Memb. 1, Subs. 1)

The very fear was enough to destroy some relationships. It is perhaps rather difficult for the modern audience or reader to appreciate fully how heinous such a deed was, because the tradition of male friendship, with its roots both in classical tradition and in companionship-in-arms, which writers from Aristotle to Montaigne had thought more important than love of woman, is no longer something with which we are at all familiar. Love and friendship were topics which Shakespeare treated frequently, both together and separately in many different ways, from the early *The Two Gentlemen of Verona* possibly to the collaborative *The Two Noble Kinsmen*, based on Chaucer's *Knight's Tale*. It is abundantly clear that he did not share Montaigne's rather reactionary and anti-feminist views, but that he valued both love and friendship, and recognized that their demands were not always so very different and that no man who could deceive his friend could be taken seriously as a true lover. In *Othello* a proper friendship with Cassio is not developed; but here in *The Winter's Tale* we are told Leontes and Polixenes were brought up together in their youth, as friends often were. (One may compare the then well-known pair, Titus and Gysippus, whose story Shakespeare would have known from Elyot's *Boke of the Governour*; his own Valentine and Proteus in *The Two Gentlemen of Verona*, and the princes in Sidney's *Arcadia*.) To the fear of the false friend Shakespeare added in *The Winter's Tale* the fear of cuckoldry, equally common in literature and life. It is, as we soon realize, a fearful and corrosive combination leading to uncontrollable passion.

Conclusion

As we have seen, many themes can be singled out by critics for treatment: some run throughout the play, others appear more briefly and are then replaced by another. Many are closely related, or may even be more or less the same as another but called by a slightly different name. This chapter has dealt with only a few of the more prominent ones. There are many others, and more material is available elsewhere in the book to help the reader to develop studies of other themes should he or she wish. For example, it has been suggested that the idea of life as some kind of artistic fiction, perhaps a play, runs through *The Winter's Tale*: the stress on the fictionality of the work is frequently remarked on throughout, especially in the chapter on structure. The chapter on sources contains a section on fortune, and both of the first two chapters deal with the pastoral elements and the contrasts between court and country.

4. Character, Speech and Style

Introductory

It was the professed aim of many Renaissance dramatists to hold the mirror up to nature which, as Hamlet tells the players, was the very purpose of playing. Indeed the most celebrated and influential definition of comedy (attributed to Cicero) described it as an imitation of life: the glass of custom and the image of truth. However, it would be a grave mistake to think that Renaissance men understood this to mean that a proper comedy should directly reflect the world around them and show on the stage a naturalistic representation of life as it was lived from moment to moment. To hold up the mirror to nature was taken to mean that the drama should reflect those general or universal truths manifest in the world, and that it should do this in such a way that the selection and presentation of material was both pleasing and instructive. Jonson wrote accordingly that comedy should be 'accommodated to the correction of manners' (*E.M.O.O.H.H.* III.6.209). The selected reflections and the distortions such an accommodation and such a view of the real implies considerably modifies any simple understanding of Hamlet's words. Shakespeare's plays have continued to be judged by their success in giving their audience what Dr Johnson later called a 'just picture of life'. Interestingly he found fault with them not because they failed to depict the real world in all its particularity, but because they lacked moral purpose, were more intent on entertaining than instructing and neglected poetic justice: it seems that for Johnson a 'just picture' would once again be a rather selective and rearranged reflection of life as we know it. For still later critics and audiences the wish for such a picture remained constant but the idea of what constituted it changed, as did perceptions of Shakespeare's success in painting it.

Praise for Shakespeare's consummate ability in the presentation of character may well mean, then, an ability to create appropriate types to illustrate a moral view of the world, or a command of techniques giving the impression of the way men really behave, or even somehow succeeding in convincing the audience of a character's psychological realism. These characteristics are not mutually exclusive and Shakespeare is often praised for being able to give us both the type and the individual voice together. Dr Johnson, for example, recognized and admired an ability to present the species rather than the individual in Shakespeare's work, something he said he rarely found in other poets. Yet this effect was partly achieved, he thought, by the use of dialogue which is so appropriate to the action it accompanies that it seems hardly to be fiction at all, but selected from the utterance of real men. The concentration on character and its importance by contrast with plot, perceived as a reflection of Shakespeare's deep and continued interest in human nature, grew.

It has so long been a commonplace that characters in a play, however real they seem in some respects, should not be treated as if their life continues when they are not on the stage, that it is not necessary to repeat it; yet it was a temptation to which some Victorian critics succumbed, developing, in the most extreme cases, fantastic curiosity about topics like the girlhood of Shakespeare's heroines, or conjectures about the size or existence of Lady Macbeth's family. (To be fair to A. C. Bradley, who is usually derided for giving space in a long note to the question of the Macbeths' children, we should note that he does remark that we cannot tell if they had any or no, 'and it does not concern the play'.) However, it is all too easy for modern writers to slip from time to time, even without noticing it, into what we may think of as the now old-fashioned habit of treating characters as if they were real people.

In his excellent introduction to the Arden edition of *The Winter's Tale*, J. H. P. Pafford begins his section on characters with a paragraph in which he writes sympathetically of Victorian critics' interest in the personalities created by Shakespeare's imagination. He suggests that while the characters 'often carry various themes . . . the personality of each character has importance whatever its other functions may be'. He uses the word 'personality' again in contrast with 'conventional character' when writing about Perdita a few pages later. The distinction he is making is, in practice, obvious to most students of the plays. On the one hand, one carefully avoids naïvely naturalistic expectations and judgements, and cultivates an awareness of the appropriate conventions of the stage; one never forgets – indeed how could one forget in *The Winter's Tale* of all plays? – that one is watching, or reading, a play. On the other hand, one does not generally think of characters simply as one-dimensional pasteboard figures, personifications such as Anger or Jealousy, or representatives of stock types, like tyrants, wronged women, lovers, old fathers, clowns, scolds and so on. This is not to say that English drama is not full of such types; indeed, examples are readily recalled, yet they frequently have a life, a vigour, a dramatic personality which can transform and transcend conventions, giving the audience a convincing illusion of their realism. It is a remarkable achievement, not least because the type seems far more in evidence in the classical dramatic tradition from which English Renaissance drama in part descended. Renaissance ideas about the relationship between the characters of fiction and the characters of life would also have tended to encourage the presentation of types. Artistic decorum required that a character should behave and speak in a way typical of all such characters, rather than in the idiosyncratic way in which one individual representative of a type might have been imagined to behave.

In his *Discoveries*, Shakespeare's contemporary Ben Jonson wrote: 'Language most shewes a man: speake that I may see thee' (Herford and Simpson (eds), VIII, p. 625). The discussion of the stage presentation of character invariably and quite properly depends a great deal on the nature and style of characters' utterances and it therefore seemed entirely appropriate to link the treatment of character and style in this chapter.

Genres, Style and Characterization

In the first chapter of this book, when the difference between comedy and tragedy was discussed, it was pointed out that dramatic theorists differentiated between the characters considered appropriate to the different kinds. Tragedy, it will be recalled, traditionally was thought to deal with historical, or apparently historical, persons of high rank – those persons, as one theorist put it, who live in the palaces of kings; while the characters of comedy were, it was said, the inhabitants of humbler dwellings with far more moderate means, playing their part in more patent fictions. Of course, as we saw, these conventional divisions were not always preserved in the comic drama of the day, which, roughly speaking, divided into romantic comedy, which is clearly fictitious but has principal characters of elevated rank, (such as *Twelfth Night*), and more realistic comedies of London life dealing with men of moderate means, and their families and servants, involved in love affairs, infidelity, cheating, hypocrisy, greed and all kinds of chicanery. Here we may see, as Jonson put it, the 'deeds and language such as men do use' (*E.M.I.H.H.*, Prologue 21), all contained in an exemplary fiction intended to edify the audience. In tragedy, if the fiction is or seems to be historical and cannot therefore be manipulated in the same way, moral lessons were nonetheless often both pointed and drawn. Not surprisingly these tend to be of a general kind: tragedy, for example illustrates the changeable nature of fortune, the instability of the fallen world, the pride, ambition and sinfulness of fallen men, and so on. Since it commonly deals in the extravagant passions of heroic figures it tends to present these in an elevated style quite different from the more down-to-earth aims of Jonsonian comedy. Here are deeds and language such as ordinary men do not use.

As we have seen, *The Winter's Tale* combines these two different genres and Shakespeare does not make many concessions in order that the two should blend together – instead he juxtaposes them. Detractors of tragicomedy frequently complained that the form was an indecorous mixture of ranks and styles. The theorists who advocated it spent time explaining how it required a careful and proper mingling of persons of different social status. The mingling parallels Guarini's theory and practice of alternation between scenes of a serious and comic nature so that the audience will always remember that it is watching a tragi-comedy, rather than either a tragedy or a comedy. Shakespeare, for reasons examined in the chapter on structure, and elsewhere, kept the two modes surprisingly separate. This is very obvious in his treatment of shepherds. Guarini had argued that shepherds in pastorals could be from all ranks since in a pastoral society there must have been a social hierarchy and so one did not have to have non-pastoral kings and nobility beside lower-or middle-class shepherds, hence avoiding hybridization of a further sort. It was another example of his wish to blend things together smoothly. Shakespeare ignores this as he ignores other things in Guarini, and although Leontes is King of a country famous for its shepherds, he does not attempt to treat his court as a pastoral court, and we see nothing of Polixenes' court; while the shepherds of Bohemia are very clearly of a lower rank (even if the old shepherd has lately 'grown into an unspeakable estate' by his good fortune), which many therefore, would have thought appropriate to a comedy. In Act V Scene 2, the characters of lower rank from Bohemia, the shepherd and his son, are described in the conversation between the gentlemen as providing evidence and witness of the identity of Perdita and a little later appear to speak of it themselves. In the gentleman's account all the attention, not surprisingly, is on the two royal families and then on Paulina; the rustics are presented as no more than types and play rather static supporting roles: '... now he thanks the old shepherd, which stands by like a weather-bitten conduit of many kings' reigns' (V.2.53–4). Earlier in the play the style of the Clown's narrative had helped to change the mode from tragic to comic, when he described those events which have now been solemnly set out at court and recounted to us by the gentlemen. Then a dialogue between rustics paralleled the opening dialogue of the play between courtiers and marked the new comic beginning. Here once again is a courtly exchange in prose.

The end of the scene when the shepherds appear is quite different. There are no gentlemen on stage. The nearest one gets to the earlier mode is with the disreputable Autolycus who claims to have served Florizel once. The Clown's account of the family reunion naturally gives a rather more intimate picture of his and his father's relations with the royal family. He is comically intent on making much of their recently acquired gentility:

> . . . I was a gentleman born before my father: for the King's son took me by the hand, and called me brother; and then the two kings called my father brother; and then the Prince my brother and the Princess my sister called my father father. And so we wept; and there was the first gentleman-like tears that ever we shed.
>
> (V.2.135–141)

This account certainly reminds us of the Clown's earlier speech on the death of Antigonus. In both cases something is very much changed by the way in which it is described. The rustics are now prominent in the account of the revelations and the description is comically involved. To the courtiers the royal families' 'joy waded in tears', a fanciful and paradoxical idea, while the old Shepherd's weeping made him seem like an ancient 'weather-bitten conduit', equally fancifully reduced to a kind of architectural ornament. Tears of emotion are for the Clown 'gentleman-like' tears, quite naturally, given his obvious pleasure in his newfound status, which engages him more than the 'deal of wonder' which has astonished the gentlemen. The emphasis which is given to being a 'gentleman born', which normally took three generations but which here is accomplished at a stroke – according to the Clown he seems to have been born again as a gentleman but four hours ago – reminds the audience that the first time we saw these rustics they had discovered something newborn. The end of the play is commonly described by some critics as providing new life or the reinvigorating of old life. The shepherds' gentility is a comic example of it.

At the end of the scene the Clown draws attention to the fact that the court, 'the kings and the princes, our kindred', as he cannot resist calling them, are going to look at 'the Queen's picture', and asks Autolycus to follow him and his father, one presumes to the house of Paulina. However, they are not in the list of characters appearing in the last scene and certainly take no part in it. So it is that Shakespeare very carefully keeps the two parts of the play distinct. The two groups of characters, shepherds and members of the royal family, are kept separate on stage, and by telling the audience about the discovery of Perdita rather than showing it, the shepherds' part in the conclusion, and even the prominence of a pastoral-romance type of solution, are somewhat diminished. We are returned as completely as possible to a court environment with as few incongruous elements as possible.

The play begins and ends in the court of Leontes in Sicilia and there the principal characters are royal or courtiers. It is an appropriate setting for a tragic action. Any doubt the audience may have, any feeling that it might also be a suitable setting for a romantic comedy – *Twelfth Night*, for example, begins at a ducal court – is soon dissipated. Leontes is struck by a sudden and consuming passion. The onset of his jealousy is not naturalistically motivated, though the effect it has on him may be charted in a manner, if not in a style, in which one can perceive the workings of the mind. The move to Bohemia in the central section of the play, as we observed when considering the structure and sources of the play, is the kind of change of place and the kind of setting one expects in certain types of comedy. Here we are reminded of the pastoral tradition, though, as we have already seen, on closer examination nothing proves to be quite as simple as it at first may seem. We appear to be in that natural, or green, world some critics write of as existing at the centre of romantic comedy. If the social status of the characters fits the theorists' prescriptions in general, there are, as often occurs in pastoral and romance, several more elevated characters in disguise. The role of the threatening father is, as we have seen, familiar in comedy, and whatever his role in the Sicilian part of the play, Polixenes fits in perfectly here. The incident of young lovers escaping together when faced by the threat is also familiar. A name with a meaning, like Perdita, is quite usual in comedy but not in tragedy. In comedy the names are made up and therefore can be used entirely decorously to indicate something about a character, whereas the names of the characters in tragedy have to seem to be historical and therefore, like the names of historical figures, do not generally tell one anything about their natures.

The appropriateness of names with meaning in comedy had been remarked on by Donatus when commenting on the practice of Terence, and there were also many instances in contemporary comedies. This must have been encouraged by the extensive and often quite serious attention which some contemporary writers gave to the idea that all names were not arbitrary signs but had a real connection with things, which originated in Plato's *Cratylus*. Shakespeare sometimes followed the comic practice of giving his characters names with meanings, for example in *The Two Gentlemen of Verona* Valentine is faithful, and

Proteus protean; in *Henry IV* Nym steals, which is the cant meaning of his name, and presumably Doll Tearsheet follows a calling which would give her plenty of opportunity to live up to hers; yet Shakespeare also makes fun of the use of such names, defeating, as he so often does, the expectation of those who expect the conventional from him. Speed in *Two Gentlemen* and Silence in *Henry IV* Part 2 are clearly ironic. Names derived from classical and perhaps mythological sources were also sometimes used by writers, bringing with them the associations of their origins. Autolycus is, as we shall see below, a case in point. He also illustrates another aspect of the discussion of genre and character-type, for while he appears in a part of the play which generally causes critics to look to romantic comedy for sources and parallels, he also has some obvious affinities with the rogues we find in rogue literature and in the stage streets of London comedies.

If the characters are carefully adapted to the genres in which they appear, what of the style? The style of the last plays has often been considered to be complex and difficult to appreciate. Some critics have expressed disappointment with it, considering it inferior to that of the mature comedies, where what the characters say and the way in which they say it has often been thought to create an illusion of naturalism by seeming to be the appropriate expression of the inner self of a developed dramatic character. In the last plays it has sometimes been observed that the language the characters use is not intended to characterize them but rather is appropriate to the nature of the prevailing situation and events. One may well think that this happens elsewhere, too, and that the distinction between the last plays and others may sometimes be exaggerated in this respect. But one should certainly not be surprised to find it happening in these plays above all others because it is what one might naturally expect in works based on romance; it is appropriate to the nature of the kind. Romances depend for their effect on a narrative which grips the attention of the reader and this is usually achieved by incident rather than the detailed depiction and delineation of character. The propriety of language to form is a major example of the profound sense of decorum discernible again and again in the last plays. It is perhaps easier to see what is happening by example than generalization.

The play opens, as Shakespeare's plays sometimes do, in the middle of a conversational exchange. This one is in prose and takes place between Camillo and Archidamus. The style and the manner of the speakers places them as courtiers as surely as what they say. When Archidamus protests to Camillo that Bohemia will seem very different from Sicilia when Camillo visits for they will never be able to provide such entertainment as the Sicilian court has provided, the expression of his courtly modesty is as elaborate as the sentiments it contains. Essentially the same style rather more elaborately extended is to be found in the exchange between the gentlemen describing the reconciliation of Leontes and Perdita. As we have seen above, these two exchanges mark out sections of the play belonging to the same genre. There are of course many examples of courtly exchanges in Shakespeare, and one might compare the language of the exchange between Kent and Gloucester at the beginning of *King Lear*, and perhaps the parody of such a style taken to extremes in the speech of Osric in *Hamlet*. This is the style that Autolycus attempts to adopt when, having exchanged clothes with Florizel, he removes his beard and pretends to be a courtier to intercept the Shepherd and Clown on their way to reveal all to Polixenes. He arrogantly catechizes them about their intentions, quibbles in a patronizing manner with what he presumably thinks of as court wit on their declaration that they are but plain men, and says of himself:

> Whether it like me or no, I am a courtier. Seest thou not the air of the court in these enfoldings? Hath not my gait in it the measure of the court? Receives not thy nose court-odour from me? Reflect I not on thy baseness court-contempt? Think'st thou, for that I insinuate, to toaze from thee thy business, I am therefore no courtier? I am a courtier cap-à-pie; and one that will either push on or pluck back thy business there; whereupon I command thee to open thy affair.
>
> (IV.4.725–33)

The speech is full of fancy words, like 'enfoldings', 'insinuate', 'toaze' and 'cap-à-pie' which Autolycus takes for courtly diction. He certainly convinces the rustics that he is a 'great courtier' and when he asks if they have an advocate to the king they are so accustomed to courtiers speaking a special language, that the Clown thinks he means that he needs to have a gift and takes the word to mean a pheasant. Autolycus's response to this is a parody of the courtier's effortless, patronizing superiority and condescension:

> How blessed are we that are not simple men!
> Yet Nature might have made me as these are:
> Therefore I'll not disdain.
>
> (IV.4.740–42)

For this pompous utterance he goes one step further and speaks in blank verse.

As has been observed, the second prose exchange in the play introduces the comic section, and the way in which the method of description can transform the impression an event makes on the audience has been treated in some detail. Such an effect was obviously paramount in Shakespeare's mind here. There is a distinct difference between the pains he takes to make the audience recognize courtly language and the parody of courtly language, and the way in which he deals with the language of the rustics. It is not as important to the play as, for example, the creation of a comic or tragic tone at the appropriate point. Throughout he is less concerned to give the old Shepherd a style consistent with his social status. This is, perhaps, partly possible because the shepherd in pastoral does not have such a clearly defined social role as, for example, the lower orders in the earlier comedies. There are, of course, many instances where a rustic tone is sought and achieved, for example, when the Shepherd discovers Perdita he says:

What have we here? Mercy on's, a barne! A very pretty barne. A boy or a child, I wonder? A pretty one, a very pretty one. Sure, some scape. Though I am not bookish, yet I can read waiting gentlewoman in the scape: this has been some stair-work, some trunk-work, some behind-door-work. They were warmer that got this than the poor thing is here . . .

(III.3.68–74)

Rusticity here resides in the use of dialect words – 'barne' and 'child' for a female baby – and the kind of jesting about sexual indiscretions reminds us of the jokes of servants in comedy. There are touches and turns of phrase throughout having the same function, but there is no consistent attempt at social realism. Shakespeare certainly does not exploit the possibilities of humour to be imagined in the utterance of one who 'from very nothing, and beyond the imagination of his neighbours, is grown into an unspeakable estate' (IV.2.38–40).

Polixenes's opening lines are far more elevated than the conversation of the courtiers. He is speaking formally and with some pomp:

Nine changes of the watery star hath been
The shepherd's note since we have left our throne
Without a burden. Time as long again
Would be filled up, my brother, with our thanks,
And yet we should for perpetuity
Go hence in debt. And therefore, like a cipher
Yet standing in rich place, I multiply
With one 'We thank you' many thousands more
That go before it.

(I.2.1–9)

The reference to shepherds of course looks forward to the pastoral part of the play which appropriately is set in Polixenes's kingdom. Molly

Mahood suggests that these orotund phrases transport the audience to the world of the player-king ('The Winter's Tale' in *Casebook*, ed. K. Muir). The style of the speech certainly does seem to give a further indication of the nature of the fictional world in which this play is set. If the dialogue between courtiers indicates that this could well be a serious rather than a comic work, the style of this speech not only seems at a further remove from a real courtly world, but hints also that we are standing on the verge of romance. The orotund style is not, however, uniformly maintained: indeed part of the scene which follows is written in a fairly colloquial style, for example the joking exchange between Polixenes and Hermione and the talk about the two princes' youth. Certainly, then, on the evidence of his subsequent speeches and behaviour, Polixenes himself is not uniformly characterized by this speech: the style – as is quite frequent in the last plays – is here more indicative of the nature of the action of the play than of the character of one of the *dramatis personae*. Later in Bohemia one may perhaps recognize some relationship between the style of his opening speech and his role as the angry, disguised king and disapproving father, but once again this is not a question of uniform characterization, but of language as a sign of role and action.

The Characters

Leontes

A reading of the characters in *The Winter's Tale* depends a great deal therefore on an understanding of genre, style and role, rather than on an attempt to give an impression of consistent naturalistic characterization. It is no good looking for any consistent psychological motivation to explain Leontes's jealousy and his subsequent behaviour towards his queen and his former friend. Because they are uncomfortable with the sudden shock of such an inexplicable change, and seek plausibility of character and incident consistent with everyday experience, critics have sometimes suggested that Leontes is already jealous when the play begins. Such an approach changes the interpretation of the actor playing the part in the opening scenes, since the jealousy has somehow to be made obvious to the audience. It makes all the references to happy family life and friendship ironic. The alternative view is that Shakespeare is economically compressing and concentrating his material to make the audience acutely aware of the mad derangement which transforms an ideal happiness into a nightmare. At first the two princes look back to an innocent youth, a time before their spirits were 'higher reared/With stronger blood' (I.2.72–3), and joke about sexual experience as a loss of innocence. Soon however, all the jokes turn sour and to Leontes the world seems no longer innocent but destroyed by infidelity and lust. The audience is at a loss to comprehend this sudden jealousy, and sees all too plainly a world of fallen humanity prey to the unexplained and inexplicable motions of the passions. The movement seems to parallel man's mythical progress from the childlike innocence of the unfallen world to the more childish passions of disillusioned maturity in a fallen world. Like the archetype, of course, this fall is grounded on error and sustained and compounded by subsequent error: Leontes wilfully rejects the words of the oracle and, preferring his own fallible judgement to that of Apollo, seems to be instantly afflicted for his pride.

Shakespeare uses a number of commonplaces already familiar to his audience to depict Leontes and allow the play to move at such speed. As has been observed in the chapter on themes, he draws particularly on the well-known tradition of male friendship, which was very familiar both in imaginative literature and in theoretical treatments in the Renaissance. There were many examples of false friends stealing their friends' ladies and so, while Leontes sudden suspicion may be psychologically implausible, it is not really quite so surprising in terms of a literary tradition. Interestingly, Leontes's suspicion seems to have been provoked by Hermione's use of the word 'friend', presumably as she gives her hand to Polixenes:

> . . . I have spoke to th'purpose twice:
> The one for ever earned a royal husband;
> Th'other for some while a friend.
>
> (I.2.106–8)

Leontes seems to understand the word to mean lover, as it often did. The travesty continues with a further confusion of conventional ideas about friendship and love: 'To mingle friendship far is mingling bloods' (I.2.109). The mingling of blood as a sign of male friendship was attested in classical literature, though it was generally thought of as a barbaric practice. There is a reference to Scythians quaffing blood to establish a 'perfect league of friends' in Campion's dedicatory poem to King James, set before the published description of the masque, in honour of the union of Lord Hayes and his bride in 1607. Sexual intercourse was also thought of as a mingling of blood according to Aristotelian physiology, so the disturbed movement of Leontes's mind may well be imagined to be putting these things together. He is quickly transformed into a jealous husband eager to destroy both friend and wife. What happens to him follows, albeit with quite extraordinary rapidity, a course set out in popular literature and indeed in medical treatises. Burton, citing a tradition dependent on Galen, writes: 'Those which are jealous, most part, if they be not otherwise relieved, proceed from suspicion to hatred, from hatred to frenzy, madness, injury, murder and despair' (Part. III, Sec. iii, Memb. 3). He records that jealousy has been called the 'fountain of murders' and has many examples of the outrages perpetrated by both husbands and wives on the mere suspicion of infidelity. Leontes's speeches are haunted by sexual imagery. Colloquial diction and rhythm are mixed with a more complex style to reflect the disturbance, the *tremor cordis* he suffers. The affectionate exchanges between father and son take on double meanings and alternate with bitter asides and obsessive digressions. The ordinary domestic context contrasts sharply and painfully with Leontes's distorted perception of reality. At one stage he seems to be trying to regain control. The style becomes formal and mannered and he tries to explain to himself in a reasoned fashion how the operation of affection, probably here meaning sexual desire, which can build on nothing and exist in dreams rather than reality, is all the more plausible as an explanation of Hermione's behaviour since, in this case, it has a real object, Polixenes. But the control is obviously forced and disturbing, as apparent rationality founded on delusion always is. Consequently it is soon lost again and Leontes's speeches run on with plays on words and sexual images. In his exchange with Camillo towards the end of the scene, Camillo is polite, clear, direct, everything one would expect of a courtier, while Leontes is, at first, tangled up:

> . . . Ha'not you seen, Camillo –
> But that's past doubt, you have, or your eye-glass
> Is thicker than a cuckold's horn – or heard –
> For to vision so apparent rumour
> Cannot be mute – or thought – for cogitation
> Resides not in that man that does not think –
> My wife is slippery?
>
> (I.2.267–73)

and then frantic:

> Is whispering nothing?
> Is leaning cheek to cheek? Is meeting noses?
> Kissing with inside lip?
>
> (I.2.284–6)

If all this is nothing, 'Why, then the world and all that's in't is nothing' (I.293). Act II

Leontes's entry in the next act coincides with the beginning of Mamillius's story, and in a moment a child's fantasies are replaced by an adult's, which are not a jot less implausible. At first he seems to exult that Polixenes's flight proves his guilt:

> ... How blest am I
> In my just censure, in my true opinion!
> (II.1.36–7)

Diseased opinion has become the truth for Leontes, and the grounds for embarking on vengeance under the pretence of self-righteous justice. It is the kind of transformation which makes the murder of Desdemona seem to Othello to be a judicial execution./Leontes is torn between two conflicting reactions. It may be satisfying to be proved right, but he at once recognizes 'how accurs'd' it is to be 'so blest'. Like Othello, he would have been happier in ignorance. The folklore he refers to to explain his condition is perhaps more revealing than he intends. Only the man who has seen the spider in the cup dies, so only the husband who knows he has been cuckolded is affected by it. Yet it is not the spider itself which poisons the drinker, only 'his knowledge' which is 'infected'. We may reflect that, in Hermione's case at least, there is no truth in the accusation of adultery, here it is the infected imagination of the 'victim' which destroys him. There is no deep or extended consideration of inward torment, something of which we get a greater impression with Othello, where imagination builds fantastically and with increasing grossness on Desdemona's supposed infidelity with Cassio until Othello is determined not to discover her innocence but rather that she should be 'proved a whore'. At the same time Othello's mind runs on his role as a military leader, eloquently expressing what he was and is convinced he now can be no more. Leontes's condition has moved much further much faster, as this comparison with the Othello of Act V demonstrates. Here the expression of the pain of knowledge is side by side with the conviction of the justice of the accusation. Of course, in a tragicomedy, there is less time to present the rather slow transformation in the mind of the hero such as we find in *Othello* but, as we have already seen, the approach to characterization is somewhat different, concentrating, as is usual in the last plays, more on the presentation of incident and action than on individual characterization.

The Leontes who thinks he is being just seems to the audience to be a tyrant. Like other tyrants he rejects good advice and counsel first from Camillo and then from Antigonus. The question of tyranny emerges in the exchange between Leontes and Paulina in Act II Scene 3, as it does in Hermione's speech at her trial. His pretence to be just is revealed for what it is when he wilfully prefers his own preconceived view to the judgement of Apollo and dismisses the oracle as false.

When the news of Mamillius's death is brought and Hermione collapses Leontes at once recognizes his guilt, and from then on his role is that of the penitent. He does not appear again until Act V. By then, Cleomenes suggests, he has 'done enough', 'performed a saint-like sorrow' and paid 'More penitence than done trespass' (V.1.1–4). Yet Leontes cannot forget, nor forgive himself. The audience is not shown evidence of change, or growth of self-knowledge in him: indeed there is not the time to do so. The Arden editor remarks on the lack of evidence that he has changed and worries that a true penitent for wife-murder would not suggest that he would murder a new wife at the prompting of Hermione's ghost, and 'worst of all is his desire for Perdita'. As has already been suggested in the chapter on the sources, the idea that Leontes experiences desire for Perdita is based on a misunderstanding of the passage. If the audience does not know *Pandosto* then it will not take Leontes's words seriously; if it does, the contrast between earnest and jest will be very obvious. The mention of a husband murdering his wife at the instigation of an apparition of her predecessor sounds rather the theme of a folk tale, or is perhaps a little like a female version of the speaker in Donne's 'The Apparition', and the words of the imagined ghost remind us of the ghost in *Hamlet*, who is also concerned about an unsuitable second marriage (see Arden notes for V.1.62 and 67). Again, the tone of the passage is crucial. Of course Leontes is meant to be taken seriously: he wishes to make it clear that he has no intention of marrying again and still feels Hermione's loss deeply, but perhaps the touch of the dramatist is a little lighter than is sometimes suggested. When Hermione's ghost is described as her spirit possessing her corpse, Pafford notes that this kind of corporeal ghost is to be found in ballads rather than in tragedy. The audience understands the whole exchange which follows not as a way of finding out something about the psychological state of Leontes's mind, but recognizes here, so often in the play, that what is being evoked is a fictional world, a world of ballads, folk tales, fantasy, and not the real world. It is one of a whole series of contributions to the sense of the old tale and, as such, it looks forward to the conclusion of the play. Once again one concludes that individual characterization is rather subordinated to the effect of the whole. As is so clearly demonstrated, the return of Perdita and the consequent restoration of Hermione is more than even the most ardent penitent deserves, and the point of the conclusion has more to do with the difference between what one deserves and gets in life and what one can get in fiction than it has to do with the psychological rehabilitation of Leontes.

Polixenes

Polixenes is clearly a much less prominent figure in the play. He fulfils the traditional role of the friend who is wronged in the first half of the play. In the second part he is again presented in a conventional role, or perhaps in two roles combined: the disguised ruler and the hostile father. It should be said that the combination may have been suggested by a comedy by John Day called *Humour Out of Breath*. There were plenty of examples of disguised rulers in contemporary literature. Perhaps the most celebrated example was the Roman Emperor, Severus, whose exploits were frequently recounted and elaborated. There is an account, for example, in Sir Thomas Elyot's *The Image of Governaunce*. Severus was a model of the ideal ruler and by his use of disguise was able to bring about dramatic revelations of the vices of his people. Several rulers in disguise appeared on the Elizabethan and Jacobean stage. There is Henry V on the night before Agincourt, and in Samuel Rowley's *When You See Me, You Know Me*, Henry VIII has comic encounters with low-life London characters. It happens, too, in John Marston's *The Malcontent* and *Fawn*, as well as in *Measure for Measure*. In these examples the device is used to expose the nature and views of ordinary men, often comically, and also to reveal with a sharper, more satirical edge prevalent social vices. Polixenes combines this role with that of the hostile father, frequently found in comedy, as demonstrated in the chapter on structure.

At first, we see him in conversation with Perdita and, like many of his prototypes, he encourages one of the lower order to reveal her views on a topic of importance in the play. Such scenes always produce dramatic irony because the audience is aware of the disguise, but the irony is more complicated here for Polixenes's views are, if considered as an expression of artistic theory, entirely in accord with those of the majority of his educated contemporaries, and contrast with the simpler views of Perdita. However, if they are considered as rules for human breeding then, as the audience is well aware, neither Polixenes nor Perdita will practise what they preach. (Their discussion has been examined in the chapter on themes.) When he casts off his disguise it is to catch a son who is 'unfilial' and, by making an unsuitable marriage, is demeaning his royal birth and not taking his dynastic obligations seriously. However serious this is to the king, and the contemporary audience would have been more aware of this than we are, no one can ever have found these young lovers to be proper targets for the revealed ruler's wrath and justice, as are the miscreants who are usually caught out: compare, for example, the sinners in *Measure for Measure* from Angelo down. Polixenes, the angry father, takes over and instead of a cool distribution of justice, he rages, threatens, sentences and then draws back before he storms out. If his anger is frightening and provides a much diminished reflection of the threat of Leontes in the first half of the play, its hyperbole is not without the hint of comedy, a hint which, as we have seen, is soon taken up and developed. Duped fathers usually had something of the ridiculous about them. This mixture is present in different proportions in Shylock, complaining about his daughter and his ducats, and in Barabas with his girl and his guilders in Marlowe's *The Jew of Malta*.

By the end of the play Polixenes has become but a supporting figure in the action. Indeed, he has very little to say and the healing of the division between the two kings, which under different circumstances might have commanded some attention, is not shown but is described and then only as a part of the gentlemen's account of the return of Perdita. As that is subordinated to the spectacular return of Hermione, so the reunion of friends is subordinated to both. It was prominent at the beginning where familiar literary precedents were called upon to assist in the compressed presentation of the sudden change in Leontes and the disintegration of his harmonious and ordered life. Polixenes is a good example of a character whose dramatic function as expressed in related roles is more important in the action of the play than any attempt at developed characterization. It would be difficult to describe what he was like without simply describing his roles.

Hermione

Despite her comparatively small part in the play, including a long absence and only a short speech at the end of the play, Hermione makes a very considerable impact on audiences and critics. It is often suggested, as Pafford put it, that here we have 'a vivid picture of a personality' (*The Winter's Tale*, Arden edition, p. lxxiii). This dramatic illusion is actually effected by presenting her in two rather different ways, as dictated by the sudden change in her circumstances. At the beginning of the play she has something in common with the assured, clever, witty heroines of comedy.

She has been accustomed to teasing and jesting, and is entirely at ease with her husband, his friend, Mamillius and her ladies.

These are scenes of domestic harmony, yet the audience is painfully aware that her confidence is misplaced, having seen it set against Leontes's asides which express his sudden, unexplained and rapidly growing suspicions and consuming jealousy. Her husband's jealousy comes as a complete shock to her. She asks in bewilderment: 'What is this? Sport?' (II.1.58). Hardly; and if it were it would be in very bad taste. Her first reaction is to treat it all as a mistake, to rebuke Leontes mildly and suggest that the error will later grieve him. When she realizes that his mind is not to be changed straightaway, she accepts her sentence as the influence of some ill planet which will change in time. It seems that no one moves to convey her to prison, for Leontes asks 'Shall I be heard?', and it is left to her to arrange her own departure. In adversity she is throughout controlled and calm, in contrast with Leontes's distraction. It is clear from what follows that no one shares Leontes's opinion of her, and the repeated praise of others confirms her worth and justified reputation.

The style of her speech at her trial contrasts markedly with that of her husband; indeed, the difficulty one sometimes has in following his train of thought, as many of the involved footnotes to editions demonstrate, may make one sympathetic to her remark: 'You speak a language that I understand not' (III.2.79). She is always lucid. As we have seen in the chapter on themes, Hermione here owes quite a lot to the tradition of the calumniated wife who remains faithful. When she is restored at the end of the play Hermione has very little to say. She blesses her daughter, Perdita, but for whose return she would have remained hidden, and asks:

> ... Tell me, mine own,
> Where hast thou been preserved? Where lived? How found
> Thy father's court? For thou shalt hear that I,
> Knowing by Paulina that the oracle
> Gave hope thou wast in being, have preserved
> Myself to see the issue.
>
> (V.3.123–8)

Paulina intervenes, saying there will be time enough for that later, for otherwise people might start asking Hermione to interrupt her joy and tell her tale, too. Of course the audience knows Perdita's story: it would be boring to hear it recounted. Obviously nothing of importance to the drama has happened to Hermione while she has been in hiding, so no account of that is needed either. On reflection, audiences and readers often think that the concealment of Hermione is one of the most unbelievable things in the play, and that it diminishes the realism of Hermione's character they had experienced in the first part of the play, reducing her to a mere instrument of the plot. The whole conclusion is also often judged to be rather contrived and unsatisfactory, and indeed the apparent harmony is questioned.

The dramatic technique here is actually quite skilful, however: Hermione directs us to Perdita whose story we know, and Paulina forestalls the questioning of Hermione by directing our attention to the joy of the conclusion. Those who have complained that Hermione does not speak to Leontes should notice how prominent their embrace is in the action. There is not much movement in this scene, and when a 'statue' which has been completely still for so long moves, comes down, embraces Leontes and 'hangs about his neck' (112), the language of gesture is very clear. In a sense, of course, those who complain that this Hermione is less real than the Hermione of the first half are right. She has not long emerged from confinement; on the stage she has only just ceased to be a statue; only now has she regained her dramatic existence. We cannot expect too much. It is right that she is to be accepted more as an instrument of the plot here, for the reality of her survival and return will not stand too much scrutiny; indeed, given our observations about the effect of the ending on the audience at the conclusion of the first two chapters of this study, it would be surprising for it to be otherwise.

Perdita

Like her mother, Perdita has comparatively few lines to speak in the play. She is very prominent in Act IV Scene 4, but thereafter says little. Yet the impression which she creates and her importance in the action far outweigh the length of time she spends on the stage and the number of words she speaks. As with the presentation of other characters, some of her impact depends upon our recognizing instantly the type she represents. We are prepared in the first two scenes of Act IV, by such different figures as Time and Camillo, for the appearance of a captivating shepherdess. The foundling whose noble birth is revealed by innate, naturally noble behaviour, and the discovery of whose true identity and restoration is a crucial part of a harmonious narrative resolution, is a familiar figure in romance. The most obvious contemporary comparison outside Shakespeare is with the shepherdess Pastorella in Spenser's *The Faerie Queene*, and this has already been discussed in connection with the treatment of grace in the play in Chapter 3. Perdita may also be compared with the heroines of the other last plays, perhaps especially with Marina and Miranda. She shares their virtue and unaffected simplicity as well as their exile, though of course Miranda is not separated from her father.

Perdita's rejection of what she takes to be artificiality, which encompasses an antipathy to face-painting and the cross-breeding of the horticulturalist, as expressed in her exchange about art and nature with Polixenes, is entirely in character. Though there is naturally irony in her opposition to a horticultural practice which might have been seen as a pattern for the relationship between the lovers, there is also a certain dramatic irony in the way in which an exiled princess's essential nature is partly revealed by a plain shepherdess's uncomfortableness 'pranked up' in festive attire, 'borrowed flaunts' she calls them (IV.4.10 and 23), only grudgingly excused by the custom of the feast. Any pretence seems to make her rather uneasy. The standard against which she measures truth and falsehood is clearly thart of the pastoral world, for she remarks that the exaggerated courtly praise bestowed on her by Florizel, whom of course she knows to be a prince, would make her think he wooed her in the false way were it not that 'the true blood which peeps fairly through' reveals him to be an 'unstained shepherd' (IV.4.149–50). Though she has complied with Florizel's acting the part of Doricles, it has obviously caused her some unease: twice she tells him that she feared how it would end (IV.4.444 and 471); and when she is called upon to disguise herself for the journey to Sicilia, her reluctance is evident: 'I see the play so lies/That I must bear a part' (651–2).

It is not at all surprising that Perdita is apparently unable to appreciate the rather sophisticated distinction between artifice and artificiality which an acceptance of Polixenes's argument would presuppose. We should not be disturbed that Polixenes seems to get the better of the argument; it is to be expected: he is skilled in argument, and she has been brought up as a shepherdess. It is silly to expect the heroine to be always and unquestionably right without qualification. Her prejudices spring from her naturalness and her natural antipathy to what she considers false; in short, they reflect what is essentially admirable about her. Her rustic qualities are also revealed in her timorousness about the difference in her rank and Florizel's – 'the difference forges dread' (IV.4.17) – and a down-to-earth and ultimately pessimistic view of the likely outcome of such a relationship (35–40). Despite the naïveté of what she says about grafting we sense that she has a clear understanding of the attitude Polixenes has to love and marriage. She cannot match Florizel's high-flown amorous protestations. She speaks of Florizel's desire for her in distinctly pastoral terms as a 'desire to breed' by her (IV.4.103), and in a metaphor from dressmaking, as cut to the pattern of her own (379). When Polixenes leaves with angry threats her reaction, bravely recounting what she should and would have said is natural, and her concern for Florizel touching (IV.4.445). Despite her forebodings she impresses Camillo with her expression of admirable patience and fortitude:

> I think affliction may subdue the cheek,
> But not take in the mind.
>
> (IV.4.573–4)

The presentation of Perdita is a very skilful combination of the ideal with the natural and down to earth.

Florizel

Florizel's role is easily recognized. He is the conventional figure of the prince or noble lover in disguise. We have seen how this deception troubles Perdita: she considers his 'swain's wearing' indecorous. Of course the prince deceives his father and then when discovered conspires with Camillo, flees in disguise and deceives Leontes. The audience tends to approve of these deceptions, and would be scarcely likely to assent to Autolycus's view that 'The Prince . . . is about a piece of iniquity' (IV.4.673–4). His actions seem essentially honest. Certainly he proves to be more honest than the mythological gods he cites as precedents for his disguising. He treats two of them with some humour:

> . . . Jupiter
> Became a bull, and bellowed; the green Neptune
> A ram, and bleated;

while the third, Apollo, is treated more seriously:

> . . . the fire-robed god,
> Golden Apollo, [became] a poor, humble swain,
> As I seem now.
>
> (IV.4.27–31)

This variation in treatment, which is Shakespeare's not Greene's, may well arise from the importance of Apollo in the play. He is the deity whose oracle is consulted and rejected by Leontes: but he is also the god of honest art which contrasts with the dishonest deceptions referred to here and manifest elsewhere in the play.

Florizel's recklessness when discovered is a characteristic which might well, under other circumstances, have also given rise to disapproval. He speaks of being heir to his affection (IV.4.478), and when Camillo urges caution – 'Be advised' – he replies:

> I am, and by my fancy. If my reason
> Will thereto be obedient, I have reason;
> If not, my senses, better pleased with madness,
> Do bid it welcome.
>
> (IV.4.479–82)

To Camillo, 'This is desperate', but Florizel insists that, since he is bound by a lover's vow, it is, rather, honesty. He is not really advocating the subjection of reason to passion. In Jorge de Montemayor's *Diana*, which Shakespeare knew, there is a pastoral dialogue in which the nature of love is discussed and the 'sage Ladie Felicia' speaks of rationality and love in the following way:

> . . . though [Love] hath Reason for his mother [it] is not therefore limited or governed by it . . . perfect love (though it be the sonne of reason) is not governed by it, bicause, there is nothing, after it is borne, that doth lesse conforme it selfe to the originall of his birth, then this doth.

She speaks of the distinction which some make between virtuous and vicious love, but suggests that both of them are characterized by 'excesse', which in the one case leads to virtuous behaviour and in the other to vice, for:

> . . . if the love, which the lover beares to the mistresse of his affections, (although burning in unbridled desire) doth arise of reason, and of true knowledge and judgement, as by her onely vertues he doth judge her worthy to be beloved . . . this kind of love (in my opinion) . . . is neither unlawful or dishonest, bicause all love . . . of this qualitie doth tende to no other end but to love the person beloved for her own sake, without hoping for any other guerdon or effect of his true, and sincere love.
>
> (J. M. Kennedy, ed. Oxford, 1968, pp. 156–8)

When he speaks of his oath to his 'fair beloved' (IV.4.489) we recognize that, however reckless his actions seem, the bond of love which underlies them is rational and sensible. Florizel's vigour here, and his jollity despite Perdita's natural timidity and foreboding, is as characteristic a sign of his rank as her modesty is of hers.

Autolycus

If Florizel's deceptions are honest, Autolycus's are not. He has some of the wiliness of Capnio, one of Dorastus's servants in *Pandosto* (on whom Shakespeare also drew for Camillo), combined with the trickery of the rogues described in Greene's Conny-catching pamphlets, and the traditional figure of the Vice from the Morality plays (see Chapter 2). His presence helps to balance any tendency to see Bohemia as an idyllic pastoral world. He is not a member of this community of shepherds, but, like those who seek spiritual refreshment in this environment, or like those who, finding themselves here by chance or design, gain by the new perspectives and opportunities the experience provides, he is a fugitive from the court – or so he says – a former servant of the prince fallen on hard times. Clearly all do not benefit or seek to benefit in the same way from their withdrawal into the green world. Autolycus's financial gains by stealing and swindling, and his success in gulling the denizens of this world, making them seem simple, gullible and often ridiculous, is a satirical commentary on the more sentimental and romantic approaches to the pastoral world, its benefits and ideal inhabitants.

In this respect, Johnson described him as 'naturally conceived' as if he were a breath of fresh air in a familiar tradition; yet he is really a development of the element of satire and comedy found in pastoral tradition from the earliest times. The comedy of his presentation should not make us forget that the incorrigible rogue is a rogue. Too many treatments of him seem to forgive his cheating a little too readily because he makes fools of his victims and the audience laughs at them. Clearly, however, his great comic vigour, his performances and his songs mitigate any unsavory impression. The fact is that we are not meant to give him too much attention especially by the end of the play. He is a fairly important functionary in the plot in Act IV because he prevents the Shepherd and the Clown from taking their fardel to Polixenes and revealing all too soon, and less willingly he furnishes Florizel with the disguise for his escape. He does not receive any real come-uppance for his misbehaviour for he is never unmasked, the action simply leaves him behind and his manipulative talents are rather curtailed. For example, having got the rustics aboard the ship he told the prince of the fardel, but neither Florizel nor Perdita was in any condition to attend to his information, as both were laid low with seasickness. All he can do is comment rather wryly that, '. . . had I been the finder-out of this secret, it would not have relished among my other discredits' (V.2.119–21).

Later he finds himself seeking the good report of the rustics he has so often gulled, though we may perhaps doubt the sincerity of his professed amendment of life.

Interestingly, Apollo, the presiding oracular deity of the play, figures in the story of Autolycus's namesake in Ovid (see pp. 32 and 46). According to the *Metamorphoses*, Autolycus was the name of the deceitful son of Mercury and Chione. He was one of a pair of twins with different fathers, for Chione conceived twice on the same night, having first been impregnated by Apollo:

> And by Apollo (for shee bare a payre) was borne his brother
> Philammon who in musick art excelled farre all other
>
> (XI, 364–5)

Shakespeare's Autolycus, then, shares the name of a master of deceitful trickery, who is the twin half-brother of one who excels in the honest arts of his father Apollo. The honesty or dishonesty of art is, of course, the basis of the exchange between Polixenes and Perdita, and there are reflections of it in Autolycus's chosen art of disguise in the play, for this can be a means both of honest and dishonest deception. The assumed finery of Perdita, Florizel's shepherd garb, and the disguises the lovers adopt to escape from Bohemia, are all innocent deceptions intended to bring about good results and of course ultimately make the conditions right for the fulfilment of the oracle. But Autolycus, who exchanges clothes with Florizel, shows how disguise can be a cover for dishonesty. When he becomes a 'gentleman' to gull the Shepherd and the Clown and pockets his false beard, we realize that we have only seen him in disguise all along. His patently incredible ballads, 'Very true, and but a month old' (IV.4.265), are further examples of his use of art to deceive and lead the credulous astray; and even when his deceits do bring good results, it is not his intention that they should (V.2.122). It is thus easy to see how he presents one of the major topics of the play.

Paulina and Camillo

This couple are often thought to be rather hurriedly married off to each other at the end of the play as a convenient way of extending the comic harmony. Actually the couple have something in common in respect of their dramatic function. Between them they manage the two parts of the plot: the return of Perdita with Florizel (though of course Camillo has no idea of the full implications of what he is doing), and the concealment and restoration of Hermione. Neither of them has any regard for their personal interest, but adhere to what is right – though in rather different ways.

Camillo is the type of the ideal courtier. At first bewildered by Leontes's jealous suspicion, he, like Kent in *King Lear*, seeks to cure his king's error:

> . . . Good my lord, be cured
> Of this diseased opinion, and betimes,
> For 'tis most dangerous.
> (I.2.296–8)

but quickly recognizing the impossibility of doing so, seems to agree to his master's suggestion that he should poison Polixenes, promising to 'fetch off Bohemia for't' (I.2.334) as long as Leontes takes back his queen to prevent scandal. He is, of course, equivocating: the expression 'fetch off' can mean not only do away with, but also rescue; and there is also no doubt a double meaning in his words, 'If from me he have wholesome beverage,/Account me not your servant' (ll. 346–7). The bluntness of a Kent would be inappropriate here, for too much apart from Camillo's own safety is at stake. One would not expect an ideal courtier to agree to such a monstrous proposal. Interestingly, this very dilemma was discussed in a conversation in that celebrated book about courtly life, Castiglione's *The Courtier*:

> And what if I be in service with a Prince who handleth me well, and hopeth that I will do any thing for him that may be done, and he happen to commaund me to kyll a man, or any other like matter, ought I to refuse to do it?
>
> You ought, answered Syr Fridericke, to obey your Lorde in all thinges that tende to his profitt and honour, not in suche matters that tende to losse and shame. Therefore yf he shoulde commaunde you to conspire treason, ye are not onely not bounde to do it, but ye are bounde not to doe it bothe for your owne sake and for being a minister of the shame of your Lorde. (p. 130)

Indeed, in the exchange it explicitly states that a man should forsake 'that service, that among good men shall put hym to shame' (p. 130). Camillo sees Leontes's proposal as reflecting a rebellion within himself, and that he seeks too to bring others into the same condition. Any of Shakespeare's contemporaries would have recognized this as a potentially dreadful political danger threatening the very order of the state itself. Laurentius Grimaldus Goslicius, a sixteenth-century writer on government, wrote 'Such are the people of every state, as are the manners of those that governe; and what mutation of manners the prince useth, the same is by subiectes followed' (*The Counsellor*, 1598, p. 65). However, no one believes Leontes and he is isolated. So it is that Camillo warns

Polixenes and takes flight with him to Bohemia, where he becomes his trusted counsellor.

In the second part of the play Camillo again deceives his master, and again the audience approves of what he does, but the circumstances are very different. In the first part, his deception rescues an honest man from the threat of a tyrant and friends are divided. In the second part his deception helps to bring about their reconciliation. In both he is acting the part of the honest and virtuous courtier, first in a tragic and then in a comic environment.

If Camillo is the truth-telling courtier who has to seek banishment, Paulina remains at court to prompt the king's conscience. She appears only when Camillo has gone and her approach to Leontes reminds us of Kent's bluntness to Lear. Like Camillo she judges Leontes to be sick, and like Kent she sees herself as a physician to his disease (compare II.3.37ff with *King Lear* I.1.166). Despite Leontes's threats the scene is shot through with humour. He treats her as a scold, a callat, a hen-pecker, a Dame Partlet, and encourages his courtiers to push her out, which sometimes makes for rather ridiculous business on the stage. Some suggest that this is an attempt to lighten the tone and point the way forward to the comic harmony of the second half, but it is certainly not like the mingling of tones proposed in the Italian theories of tragicomedy. The humour is rather uneasy here, for Leontes is dangerous and childishly ridiculous at the same time. He rages, treating Paulina in a patronizing way as the unruly wife a husband cannot control, blaming Antigonus for her behaviour in a tone of petulant exasperation: 'I charged thee that she should not come about me./I knew she would' (II.3.43–4), and accusing him of setting her on. Within two scenes a striking reversal has been effected, and instead of Leontes seeking to rid himself of her, she becomes the remembrancer of his injustice.

Those critics who are concerned about consistency of character and motivation, and who tend to consider characters in plays as if they were like real people in this respect, are often disturbed by Paulina's willingness to swear that Hermione is dead when she is not. It is sometimes suggested that she must indeed believe her to be so when she returns in such grief after the queen has collapsed. Of course it is imperative that the audience believes her to be dead then. When the deception is discovered, most people in the theatre have been so amazed by the apparent transformation of a statue into a queen that the fact that there is an explanation of Hermione's survival which does not depend on magic is something of a relief. It can be accepted on the same footing as all the other extraordinary discoveries and reunions that seem such a cause of wonder to those on the stage, but which fulfil an expection in the audience that has been growing ever since it witnessed the discovery of the infant Perdita. Very few at this stage return to ponder the question of what Paulina was meant to believe. It is a very clear example of Shakespeare's primary interest in the action rather than in characterization. It is more important that Leontes and the audience should believe absolutely that Hermione is dead than to provide Paulina with a convincingly naturalistic character, consistent throughout the play.

In the last scene Paulina may, in a sense, be said to play the part of the greatest deceiver in a play of deception and deceivers. If the honest mythological counterpart of Autolycus was Philamon (see above), skilled above all others in the art of music, then Paulina is the faithful servant of the gods' 'secret purposes' (V.1.36), and practises 'an art/Lawful as eating' (V.3.111). Her art is not unlike that of the dramatist or dramatic presenter. There is nothing magical or dishonest about it. She convinces her stage audience with her spectacle, suspending and then allowing their disbelief, like a conjuror who first does a trick and then reveals how it is done. What is done – the restoration of Hermione – has what passes here for a natural explanation; how it is done is a matter of contrivance, of her art. Paulina is thus the immediate cause of an event in the play which, as we have seen when examining it from different perspectives, makes the audience consider the nature and function of artifice, especially in drama, and its relation to the non-fictional world. The audience on the stage is convinced by her, the audience in the theatre is, of course, at one more remove from the action, for the Paulina who is a real figure in the Sicilian court is for them fictional. If she is the artist's surrogate she is also his creation and his creature.

This account of characterization depends very much on identifying the types behind the characters, their part in the pattern of the plot, and their appropriateness to the dramatic kind in which they are found. It should be obvious, however, that they do not, generally speaking, give a flat, one-dimensional, etiolated impression. The vigour of local expression and the naturalism of detail does create something of a naturalistic effect, and this has sometimes tended, as has been noticed from time to time, to make audiences think of these dramatic figures as if they had an existence and importance independent of the plot. It should, however, be observed that in Shakespeare's work, and certainly in his comedies, the outcome of events, when examined closely, proves never to depend on character, or the interaction between characters alone, but rather on the manipulation of events effected by the dramatist's art, expressed in the operation of chance or accident, or the intervention of the wonderful, or the surprising, or the improbable, for example. Characters are seen by the audience as players within a dramatic tradition, and there is no illusion of being 'God's spies' looking at a simulacrum of the real world. One of the most surprising and impressive things about *The Winter's Tale*, when considering the relationship between character and plot, is what a strong impression of vigorous and naturalistic characterization can be created in a very small space, for most of the parts are very short. Close examination shows how one replaces another in the plot to create, by the end, a composite effect which reflects and expresses the structure, themes and meaning of the play.

5. *The Winter's Tale* in the Theatre

This chapter will be divided into three sections. The first will give some account of the theatrical context in which the play would first have been performed, the second will sketch its stage history and the third will discuss the play on the stage today, referring to some recent performances.

The Theatre in Shakespeare's Time

If we expect a single and simple answer to an enquiry about the nature of the Jacobean stage we will be disappointed. We should think how difficult the question would be for us to answer about the modern theatre, where, at least, the theatres are still standing and well documented. It would be difficult nowadays as one would first need to ask a supplementary question to find out which theatre the questioner wished to know about because it is patently obvious even to the least attentive members of an audience that one theatre is often very different from another. They may differ considerably in size. Many theatres still have a proscenium arch and the play takes place within a kind of giant picture frame which is, or could be, closed off from the audience by a curtain. Some have an apron stage, and there are a few where the stage is in the middle and the audience all round it. There are of course attempted reconstructions of Shakespeare's theatre, and theatres which do not attempt to reconstruct accurately but which try to give some sense of a similar space and a similar relationship between actor and audience. All these factors naturally influence both the productions and our experience of them. The stage conditions, and presumably the productions (to use the modern term very loosely), and the reaction of the audience in the Elizabethan and Jacobean theatre were likewise not uniform. If it is the Globe which springs to mind as Shakespeare's theatre, we should remember that his plays were performed not only in public theatres in London, but in the Inns of Court, at the royal court, and later in his career at the smaller indoor Blackfriars theatre. Until 1600, when it was prohibited, some large inns in the city with courtyards and galleries were used for performing plays, and one of the theatres outside the city, the Red Bull, Clerkenwell, had been converted from an inn. In the provinces plays were performed in the halls of great houses by actors on tour and the courts of inns also served as venues.

The first recorded performance of *The Winter's Tale* by the King's Men was at the Globe on 15 May 1611. It was performed at court on 5 November in the same year and was no doubt also performed at the Blackfriars. The Globe had been built in Southwark, outside the jurisdiction of the City authorities, who tended to be hostile to the theatre, in 1599. Our evidence for its appearance and facilities must be to some extent conjectural. It is partly based on what we know of the staging of plays performed there. A copy of a sketch of the Swan made in 1596 by Johannes De Witt is the most celebrated, because the most detailed and debated, piece of evidence we have of the appearance of the inside of a public theatre of the same general design as the Globe. Then there is Wenceslaus Hollar's panoramic view of the Bankside published in his *Long View of London* (1644) showing the outside of the second Globe, built on the foundations of the first, which burnt down when smouldering wadding from a cannon fired during a performance of *Henry VIII* lodged in the thatch. The builder's contract survives for the Fortune theatre, which was built early in 1600 by the builder who also constructed the Globe the year before (though unlike the Globe, the Fortune was square within and without). There is also a surviving contract for the Hope, but that was not built until 1613–14. It was polygonal and had a removable stage as it was designed to accommodate bear- and bull-baitings as well as plays. The design of the Globe itself was doubtless similar to that of open amphitheatres for animal-baiting. Though the debates continue about a number of the elements of the design there is general agreement about many of the more important features. There was, it is to be presumed, a central open yard surrounded by galleries on three levels with a platform built out from one side. The stage dimensions are calculated to be forty-three feet wide by approximately twenty-seven feet from back to front, on the evidence of the Fortune, and there was a trap in the stage certainly big enough for two men to go through at the same time. Behind the wall from which the stage projected was a 'tiring house' or dressing room, and in the wall were two doors and very probably, though not certainly, a third affording entrance to the stage. Curtains or hangings across one of these doors, or across a recess in the wall of the tiring house were sometimes pulled back, or so it seems from the apparent requirements for staging some of the extant Globe plays, to 'discover' (the word which is used in stage directions) a tableau or static display. It was not an inner stage, for no action took place there; had it done so, it would have been out of sight of many of the audience. This is where Ferdinand and Miranda are 'discovered' playing chess at the end of *The Tempest*. Above was a gallery, perhaps divided into sections by partitions, which was used as occasional additional acting space when action above was called for in the play. It was in no sense a regular second stage, often only a part of it would have been required and it was always used by a small number of actors and only for short periods. For example, a space for a window was probably all that was needed for *Romeo and Juliet*, though a little more would have been necessary in *Richard III* when Richard appears 'aloft, between two bishops' (III.4) in an attempt to get the support of the citizens. Sometimes this space may have been occupied by musicians and at others partly or wholly by spectators, depending on the demands of the play. It has been suggested that this may have been where the 'lord's room' was (which Jonson described as 'over the stage') at the Globe: a place from which distinguished or high-paying spectators could watch, set apart from the ordinary audience. Above the stage there was a cover, the 'heavens', supported by columns, with a small building above it known as a 'hut'. From this, machinery for flying effects and descents must have been operated through a trap door in the 'heavens'. The auditorium accommodated about 3,000 spectators.

Theatres like the Globe were 'public' playhouses catering for an audience similar to the one which enjoyed the animal-baiting which shared the space at the Hope. There were also indoor 'private' theatres like the Blackfriars. This hall, in a wealthy part of the city to the west of St Paul's, had been bought for £600 and adapted by James Burbage, the builder of the first London playhouse, the Theatre, in 1596. Companies of children had played on the site previously and, while prepared to accept this, influential residents would not tolerate common adult players and so, after their father's death, Burbage's sons leased it to boy companies for some eight years. When they repossessed it in 1609 a group was set up, including Shakespeare, to run it as an alternative to the Globe. A pattern was established of playing at the outdoor house in summer and at Blackfriars in winter. If it is difficult to be sure what the Globe was like, our knowledge of Blackfriars is even more scanty. Reconstructions vary considerably but it is likely that the stage was set up on one of the narrow walls of the hall, which was sixty-six feet by forty-six feet, and it would therefore have been considerably smaller than the stage in the public theatre: about twenty-six feet by sixteen feet has been suggested. We do not know how the seats were arranged, but what evidence there is suggests that there were at least two galleries, and there would have been room for three, around the walls, and boxes adjacent to the stage. The seats and galleries may have been set at angles to afford a better view of the stage. Ten spectators were allowed to sit on stools on the stage itself where they could presumably display themselves as well as see the play. There was a tiring house with a façade at the back of the stage and this must have been similar to the arrangement in a public theatre, though it may have been more elaborate. It seems to have had three doors or openings; the central one may have been a double door which, if curtained, could have been used as a discovery space. There would have been a 'heaven' above as descents and flights were not uncommon and there was a gallery for actors, musicians or lords as required. The lighting would have been artificial. Other early seventeenth-century private theatres seem to have been similar in design. In all of them the audiences were much smaller and the price of admission six times higher than in the public theatres.

It is obvious that the two theatres catered for audiences of different social classes and, since the kind of theatre built after 1600 was of the smaller, private sort, clearly players looked increasingly to the wealthy – the upper classes and the court – to provide their income. Yet the taste of both audiences was, it seems, very similar. Plays were regularly transferred from the Globe to the Blackfriars. It has been argued that the new smaller and more intimate indoor theatre with a sophisticated audience was responsible for a change in the type of play written by Shakespeare, but this can be exaggerated. The last plays grow convincingly out of work he was doing well before the move and, however he was affected by it, he would also have been conscious that the plays he wrote had to be acceptable on both stages. It would no doubt have been much easier and more effective to provide the 'solemn music' called for in *The Winter's Tale* and other late plays at Blackfriars only, but they obviously did it at the Globe too. The behaviour of the audience and the staging would have been rather different in some respects in the two places. The Globe would have been much noisier and consequently, for example, any musical effects would have been more strident. Indeed, here the entertainment would have begun and ended with jigs and farces, while at Blackfriars music was played before the play and between the acts. Stage fights, shooting off guns and any vigorous activity would have had to be very much reduced on the smaller stage.

On neither the public nor the private stages was it the practice to use scenery. The setting was unlocalized and only what characters said indicated where the scene was supposed to be taking place. Companies did, on the other hand, own quite extensive collections of properties. There were clothes, some of which were fairly grand and would have made a considerable impact on the audience when worn in the procession, which was a popular way of turning drama into spectacle. There were objects to be carried like weapons, shields, sceptres, tridents, fans, musical instruments, even the severed heads of animals and men. Whether the bear in *The Winter's Tale* was made up of one of the animal heads and skins, which no doubt the King's Men, like the Admiral's Men, had amongst their properties, we do not know for certain. There was furniture to be brought on and off stage, probably in a way quite similar to the practice in many modern theatres, where stage hands bring on a table and the actor brings his chair or papers with him. There were even tombs and trees and the like if these were required for a special part in the play, though trees would not have been used in any number even when a scene was set in a forest, and in 1598 the Admiral's Men seem only to have had one rock. Philip Henslowe's account of the goods owned by this company includes, amongst the rest, the tomb of Dido, a hell mouth, a bay tree, a tree of golden apples and a tree for Tantalus. There were stage effects, too. In the prologue to his *Every Man In His Humour* Jonson speaks disparagingly not only of the structure of plays with romantic plots, but of the effects which characterize them. Perhaps in *The Winter's Tale* the 'roul'd bullet' was heard 'To say, it thunders', and the 'tempestuous drumme' was used 'to tell you when the storme doth come'.

In the public theatre up until the end of the first decade of the sixteenth century, the staging would have been continuous: there were no intervals and the delivery of lines was very rapid, a play taking perhaps two, or at the most little more than two and a half hours. There would, no doubt, have been considerable noise and movement among those standing round the stage for the actors to cope with. It would all astonish a modern audience, and the experience of this kind of theatre for an 'everyman' in their audience is one which it is impossible to recreate, because what, to them, seemed normal is so extraordinary to us. We are used to sitting down and watching in a comparatively quiet, dry and warm theatre, and usually being given more help by designers and directors, while a play of any length without an interval makes the audience very uncomfortable. In the private playhouses, while the stage presentation would have been similar, if a little more subdued given the size of the stage, the conditions for the smaller and higher paying audience would have been rather more civilized. Here the divisions between the acts were marked by music, and this was a practice which seems to have spread to the public stage by 1610.

The Winter's Tale, like many other plays, was performed at court, and this is the third major stage to be described, though perforce in only the barest detail. The conditions, in general, were almost certainly not unlike those in the private theatres. Plays were put on at the Palace of Whitehall in the Hall, the Great Chamber, the Banqueting House, and the Cockpit, converted for playing at the expense of Prince Henry in 1611. There were also performances from time to time at other royal palaces: at Greenwich, Hampton Court, Richmond and Windsor. We know that tiers of seats were erected at Whitehall and these were divided into boxes and there was a stage built on one wall. It is referred to as being in the middle of the Hall in 1601 but it is not clear how the seats were arranged around it. Though some scholars once speculated that performances may have been 'in the round', this is not accepted now. There is an extant design for a temporary arrangement to accommodate a performance in the Hall at Christ Church, Oxford in 1605, and this seems likely to have been similar to the stages and seats set up at court. The design is very like that postulated for Blackfriars. There is not much evidence for any of the venues for court performances until a little later, and then only for the new Banqueting House, built by Inigo Jones in 1622 and used for masques until 1635 when the king stopped them lest candle smoke damaged the newly installed Rubens ceiling, and for the same architect's replacement for the Cockpit, known as the Cockpit-in-Court, finished in 1630. Court revels normally began on 1 November and continued until the beginning of Lent, and plays were performed mostly during the twelve days of Christmas, though not on Christmas Day itself. Although there had been court performances under Elizabeth, the number grew considerably under James. Shakespeare's company, the Chamberlain's and then the King's Men, which was the most popular, put on thirty-two court performances between 1594 and 1603 and 175 between 1603 and 1616.

The status, prestige and financial stability of the companies of players had obviously grown considerably since the middle of the sixteenth century. They never entirely escaped from the hostility of Puritans and the City authorities, who saw them all as no better than rogues, whores, pimps, thieves and cheats leading the young into all kinds of improvidence and immorality. Even the statute of 1572, which had required companies of players to be authorized by a patron of, at the least, the status of baron, or by two Justices of the Peace if the players were to escape being classed as beggars or vagabonds and punished accordingly, though it did sort out the sheep from the goats, could never satisfy critics with a rooted moral objection to any kind of theatrical performance. Not even the limiting of the power of authorization to noble patrons alone, which happened in 1598, nor royal protection which was granted for the first time by patent to the Earl of Leicester's company in 1574 could do that.

Shakespeare's name first appears in connection with the Chamberlain's Company in March 1595 when he was paid for performances at court in December 1594. We do not know for certain with which company he was associated before then. The Chamberlain's Company had been formed with the patronage of the Lord Chamberlain, Henry, Lord Hunsdon, and Shakespeare certainly seems to have been one of the eight sharers (that is, a member of the company who paid the expenses and received the profits, and hired the temporary players) in this company in 1596, and remained so until Queen Elizabeth died in 1603 when the company became the King's Men by letters patent and the number of sharers was increased to twelve. It was commercially very successful and Shakespeare was intimately involved in all aspects of the enterprise: he was playwright, actor and shareholder. This meant of course that he had a far greater say in how his plays were treated by the company. Many writers were under contract or were independent and sold their plays where they would or could. The plays then became the property of the company whose sharers would direct how it was to be prepared for the stage. The repertory system they operated required a large number of plays, many of which were performed only a few times and have since been lost. While Jonson published his plays in a fine large folio edition, this was an exception; most were never in print. Even Shakespeare seems not to have had an interest in publication. Companies may have given a new play every day, six days a week. When at its height, the Admiral's men performed between thirty-two and thirty-eight plays in a season. The pressure on writers and actors alike must have been very considerable. The principal roles seem to have been played by the sharers, minor roles by hired men, and women's parts by indentured boys. The sharers usually rented their playhouse and often also had to borrow money to buy the properties and to finance the running of the company. The owner of the playhouse customarily took his payment as a proportion of the takings from the gallery, and the proportion was larger if he had provided the money for costumes or properties or anything of the kind. It was unusual for a company to be able to afford to finance its own purchase of properties as the King's Men did. Some but not many sharers had a financial interest in the house in which they performed, as had Shakespeare with some of his fellows in the Globe and the Blackfriars. Most members of the theatre consequently did not make a great deal of money. Edward Alleyn, who ranked with Burbage as the most famous of Elizabethan actors, and who was a manager and an astute business man as well, was an exception, as, of course, was Shakespeare. These men, through their talents, skill and business acumen, made considerable fortunes and achieved some social status.

The Stage History of *The Winter's Tale*

The Winter's Tale enjoyed the favour at least of a sophisticated court audience in the years between its first appearance on the stage and the closure of the theatres in 1642, for of the eight recorded performances, seven were at court. However, when the theatres re-opened after the Restoration it was neglected, and there is no record of a performance until 1741. In the second half of the century it became popular once again, but, being the age of adaptation, chiefly in versions which shortened the play and concentrated on the Bohemian second part, sometimes even leaving out Leontes and Hermione altogether. Garrick's version, first staged at Drury Lane in 1756, was revealingly called *Florizel and Perdita: A Dramatic Pastoral.* It was set entirely in Bohemia, and what happened in Sicilia, that is, the contents of the first three acts of Shakespeare's play, was conveyed to the audience by way of a dialogue between Camillo and a Gentleman. Leontes was brought to Bohemia by a storm, Paulina earlier having fled thither to save her life, and it was in Bohemia that she was supposed to have had the statue made, so that when Leontes arrived he was able to see it. In general, Shakespeare's play was rendered more emotional and sentimental. Garrick played Leontes, and his performance, and indeed that of the other actors, was admired even by those who had reservations about his tampering with the text. Other versions also appeared, though Garrick's was still being performed sixteen years later; there was one without Autolycus, and there was even an operatic version of the sheep shearing.

In the nineteenth century came a progressive return to Shakespeare's text. The play proved quite popular with the celebrated actor–managers of the day: Kemble played Leontes with Mrs Siddons as Hermione at Drury Lane in 1802 and produced it several times in the next decade; Macready and Helen Faucit took the parts at Covent Garden in 1837 and thereafter. Helen Faucit's performances, especially of the final scene, in 1847 and 1848 received the highest praise. The *Glasgow Herald* recorded that: 'So complete was the illusion, so still the figure, so sightless the eyeballs, that you seemed insensibly to forget it was a living being who stood before you: and when amidst the melody of music, she turned her head towards the king, the whole house started as if struck by an electric shock, or as if they had seen the dead arise.' The praise of this part of the performance accords with a change of focus clearly apparent by the middle of the century. The interest of producers and of the audience and critics no longer concentrated on the pastoral part of the play but was now more likely to fix on the statue scene. At all events it was now re-established in the repertoire of major companies and there were a number of productions thereafter, the most remarkable of which was without doubt that by Charles Kean which began a run of 102 consecutive performances at the Princess's Theatre on 28 April 1856. Kean was a stickler for historical accuracy, not, that is, for giving his productions an Elizabethan or Jacobean character, but for a period setting and detail appropriate to the subject of the play. He was not entirely successful: for example, the corseted female shape and the crinoline proved impossible to change as much as would have been necessary – it was a question of current standards of decency as much as of custom. However, Kean set about studying heraldic records for the coats of arms for his production of *King John* in 1852, and Holbein's portraits for the costumes for *Henry VIII* in 1855. He combined this antiquarianism with a taste for spectacle on the grandest scale, building a huge Tudor hall for *Henry VIII*, ancient Athens for *A Midsummer Night's Dream* in 1856, and the London of 1399 for *Richard II* in 1857. It was said of the latter that had a fourteenth-century citizen of London seen it he would have recognized it down to the smallest detail.

His production of *The Winter's Tale* was just as spectacular. Following Thomas Hanmer in his edition of 1744 he changed Shakespeare's Bohemia into Bythinia, and developed a contrast between a classical Greek Sicilia and a more exotic Eastern setting for Bythinia. As usual, the costumes and the settings were amazing: there was a brief opening scene set before the temple of Minerva and the fountain of Arethusa; then a royal palace with musicians, slaves, and thirty-six young girls dressed as warriors dancing a Pyrrhic dance; the trial of Hermione was set in the theatre at Syracuse; and, most spectacular of all, Time was presented as a classical figure preceded by a representation of Luna in her car accompanied by personifications of the stars and followed by Phoebus rising in his chariot. The Mamillius in this production was the nine-year-old Ellen Terry; in 1906, fifty years afterwards, she played Hermione at His Majesty's Theatre in London. Though extravagant and spectacular productions have taken place since, there has, fortunately, been nothing to rival Kean's. In 1887–8, the parts of Hermione and Perdita were doubled by Mary Anderson (something which did not happen again until the production by the Royal Shakespeare Company at Stratford in 1969 when Judi Dench played both roles, as did Penny

Downie in 1986). She was much admired in both parts and especially for her dancing as Perdita, and as Hermione in the trial and statue scenes.

In 1912 everything changed when Granville-Barker produced the play at the Savoy. It was the beginning of a series of productions performed on an apron stage encouraging a greater intimacy between actor and audience, with a minimum of clutter, limited and slightly more stylized scenery, and clear, hard overhead lighting, rather than footlights. It was possible for this kind of production to move along at a pace impossible for one with more old-fashioned staging where changing the scene took time. Consequently a more complete text could be used, and that was what Barker wanted anyway for, without trying to be authentic in an antiquarian way, he was certainly trying to confront his audience with the experience of Shakespeare's play itself. The production had a mixed reception, but whatever critical and artistic success it had, it did not please large audiences and only ran for six weeks. However the effects of this radical change are still apparent today. The play was produced a number of times in the first half of this century, perhaps most notably by Peter Brook in 1951, with an impressive cast including John Gielgud, Diana Wynyard, Flora Robson and Virginia McKenna. It was performed at Stratford in 1960 but then not again until 1969, when Trevor Nunn remarked in a programme note that the late plays, with the exception of *The Tempest*, were rarely performed. Since then *The Winter's Tale* has been performed by the Royal Shakespeare Company in 1976, 1981, 1984 and 1986, so that is really no longer true. In the next section of this chapter I shall refer to some aspects of these productions when discussing the relationship between staging and understanding.

The Winter's Tale in the Theatre Today

A play only has real life when the action is staged and the lines are spoken by actors impersonating the *dramatis personae*. Theirs is a necessary intervention between text and audience which has no parallel in the relationship between the reader and the text of a novel. Consequently no student of the drama can afford just to read a play and study its text, ignoring any consideration of drama in performance. Indeed it appears that Shakespeare and certainly many of his contemporaries were not concerned to put their work in print but to put it on to the stage, and therefore to study the printed text alone is rather perverse. For the director the text is a script to perform, and this has always been the case right through the history of stage productions of Elizabethan and Jacobean plays. It may be treated with anything from reverence to cavalier disregard. In the theatre of Shakespeare's time the book-keeper was the member of the company who came the nearest to performing a director's role. He was responsible for putting in proper stage directions, arranging properties, seeing that players were ready when their cues came, but not for the principal functions of the modern director such as giving the play some overall imaginative design or direction, or finding in it some governing idea and making sure that it is made manifest on the stage. There is some evidence, though not a great deal, that Shakespeare may have been involved in details of the staging of a few of his earlier plays, and, considering his financial stake in the theatres where his later works were performed, perhaps it is to be expected that he would have maintained some interest. It is doubtful, however, if most of his contemporary writers would have had any say at all. We do not know how many alterations a book-keeper would have made to an author's manuscript in preparing it for the 'two hours' traffic of the stage', nor how much variation there might have been from one performance to another. We have already seen how much some productions of *The Winter's Tale* altered the play in the eighteenth century. What the author intended was never a very prominent consideration in the sixteenth century, nor has an attempt to recover it been very prominent in many productions since.

It can indeed be rather risky to attempt to do so. Everyone seems to have an opinion about this matter and everyone is sure his or her opinion is correct. When, in a programme note about the last plays in 1969, Trevor Nunn hazarded the hardly novel suggestion that *Pericles* had an allegorical level and was to do with a search for love through suffering and redemption, Milton Shulman in a review in the *Evening Standard* declared that such an interpretation would have given Shakespeare 'hilarious hysterics'. Clearly they each had a different but equally firmly held view of what the author intended. In a sense all productions are critical interpretations of a kind, and may well reveal the ideas and interests as well as the preoccupations of the director and perhaps of his times. These may be interesting and may also be relevant to an understanding of the play. The very choice of which plays to present in a season sometimes reflects a perception of their relevance to contemporary audiences, and the ways in which they are treated show the director's understanding of that relevance. It is doubtful whether any one production can or should be seen as definitive. Most will illuminate something in the play and, if they do no more, will set one thinking.

Some questions about plays can be answered by reference to our knowledge, where it is sufficient, of the stage practice of Shakespeare's time. However, despite modern scholarship and reconstructions of Elizabethan theatres, we are not and never can be an authentic audience. It is therefore to contemporary productions that we must turn. In what follows I shall examine aspects of certain more recent productions, paying especial attention to the ways in which they have attempted to handle some of the things which concern critics when studying the text, to try to establish their importance in the theatre.

The first thing that strikes the modern audience is something that would not have struck a Jacobean audience at all, but would have made an even greater impact on someone witnessing a production by Kean, and that is the setting of the play. It provides a director with an opportunity of suggesting, if he wishes, an attitude to the play and of persuading his audience to view it from his perspective. In *The Winter's Tale* it is possible to attempt a kind of metaphorical contrast between the Sicilian and Bohemian settings. There are, of course, problems in establishing some kind of overall consistency of style and managing the return to Sicilia at the conclusion. The production at Stratford in 1969 began with a set piece. The dark stage, illuminated only fitfully by flashes of light, was dominated by the figure of a spread-eagled man turning round and round while enclosed in a mirrored box to the sound of the displaced opening words of Time's speech. The same box was later used by Time himself in Act IV, and again in Act V for Hermione's statue. The point the director is making is obvious, perhaps even rather laboured. In a programme note Trevor Nunn wrote that 'Leontes is in a destructive nightmare, "performed" in a "wide gap of Time"' until 'spring breaks through the grip of winter, love returns, enabling Leontes to . . . be redeemed'. The opening scene was a white-floored room, dominated by a white rocking horse, and with white boxes full of toys. It was clearly a stylized nursery. Here, while a musical box played – a sound which was to echo later in the play – Leontes, dressed in white, rode his son's rocking horse. Some of the toys were used in the following action, particularly a large spinning top, the distinctive hum of which was certainly obtrusive and seemed eerie to one and melodious to another commentator. Like Leontes, all his family were dressed in white, while courtiers and servants were in black and grey and Polixenes in red. The setting had its roots in the references in the play to the innocence of childhood, and emphasized the contrast between that and the jealousy and suspicion of the adult world. In a different sense Leontes's behaviour seemed childish, contrasting with the childlike behaviour of Mamillius, and to some this suggested that Nunn was perhaps putting forward a Freudian explanation of the king's condition.

The 1976 production at Stratford directed by Nunn in collaboration with John Barton was set in the far north and in the programme much play was made of the importance and nature of the festivals to celebrate winter and summer solstices to the inhabitants of these climes. The stage was floored with bare planks and there were woven rugs and hangings round the stage with outline designs on them depicting family groups, animals, weapons, and hunting scenes. The costumes were appropriately warm, heavy, fur-trimmed, and the predominant colours orange, red and gold, Leontes alone distinguished by his simple dark brown dress. There was a leafless twisted tree trunk rising up on stage throughout, presumably reminding us of the deathly season outside what seems, at first, to be a warm and secure home.

The 1980 BBC television production by Jane Howell belonged to a rather different tradition: Dom Homfray's design was composed of cubes and cones, a stylized tree, and two large wedge shapes forming a passage down which characters entered. The set was white, and had a white tiled floor with a subdued pattern at the beginning, and, while it later changed in colour and detail, it remained essentially abstract. The costumes were generally in a subdued Renaissance style, with only Leontes really standing out wrapped in heavy, dark fur. The setting here was, without a doubt, intended to emphasize the artifice and the unreality of the tale. In 1981 this was done in Ronald Eyre's production at Stratford by showing the costumes to be worn by the actors on tailor's dummies at the beginning. Presumably the point was to acknowledge publicly that the whole thing is a performance in which actors don clothes and fictional identities. The device parallels the repeated reminders of fictionality in the play itself. This production continued with a display of artifice as spectacular as the dummies were ordinary and low-key, a pageant of Time. Touches of the nursery were still found on this Leontes, who carried a toy trumpet as he accompanied the revellers. The pageant prefigured the ensuing action, containing courtiers, rustics, a huge bear and a figure of Time from the folds of whose garment Mamillius emerges, like the New Year. All seemed festive and harmonious. It may be that the emergence of new life from the old year was meant to represent the process by which time eventually brings forth truth in the play, but this is not very obvious. The setting itself was rather unobtrusive and unlocalized: a wooden floor and tall vertical panels and the costumes white and grey and rather nineteenth-century in style.

In 1986 the predominant colour in the opening scene was white once again. The opening exchange between Archidamus and Camillo was, as it often is – though not in the television production – reduced very considerably and the two kings, Hermione and Mamillius and the court came in from playing in the snow. There was a giant polar bear rug which suggests that we are far to the north of Sicily and also hints that, later on, Antigonus will encounter this beast reincarnate, or at least one of his relatives. Not one of these productions is obviously set in Sicily. It is interesting that in the eighteenth century an editor was so concerned that Bohemia had no sea coast that he changed the name of Polixenes's kingdom, and this change was made on the stage; but now, without making any change of name, Sicily (a country whose climate is more familiar than the geography of Bohemia has probably ever been to anyone in Britain) can be treated as arctic. Whatever significance Shakespeare thought a Sicilian setting had, and remember he changed his source here, that significance is lost on modern directors and audiences, and so directors seek to transform Leontes's kingdom into a metaphor which will illuminate, in some way, the meaning of the opening of the play. Quite often there is an attempt to prefigure what will happen by some opening device, and to do this the first scene in the text – which I noted in the chapter on structure was intended to parallel the conversation between Shepherd and Clown at the beginning of the second part of the play – is frequently cut.

Though some of the productions I have described have worked well, as have others which have taken the same direction, it must be remembered that what is frequently happening is that one of Shakespeare's structural patterns is being disrupted and replaced by a director's because he considers that it will be more meaningful to the audience.

One of the most difficult and crucial decisions for the director comes quite early in the play. He has to decide how to deal with Leontes's jealousy. It is a problem which is all the more acute where the style chosen for the production, or in the case of television, the medium itself, is particularly naturalistic. A great deal is going on at the start of the play. We hear all about the great friendship of the two kings and we see Leontes apparently become suspicious and his suspicions grow to murderous proportions in a very short space. In a sense this demonstrates the frantic speed of such a dangerous and all-consuming passion. But so much has to be got into so short a space that it appears unnatural and seems to demand a stylized treatment at odds with the naturalistic performance style, the attempt to achieve an impression of psychological realism that actors now seem generally to favour. The television production handled this by a careful use of close-ups so that a slight reaction, invisible even on a small stage, could be made to register surprise, uneasiness or mental pain, for example. Whispering or speaking in a low voice direct to the camera in the soliloquies also gave a sense of intimacy. A straightforward reading of the play was attempted and worked well. At Stratford in 1960, on a proscenium stage where such intimacy was impossible, Eric Porter convinced critics of the plausibility of Leontes's growing jealousy by his understanding of the acting style necessary to simulate naturalism on such a stage and by the very careful direction of movement and reaction. In both the 1969 and 1976 Stratford productions lighting was used to emphasize the jealous reactions of Leontes. In 1976 Leontes was illuminated while everyone else was almost in the dark. In 1969, even more remarkably, the other characters were illuminated with stroboscopic light in which they were frozen, or at one point Polixenes and Hermione mimed what Leontes described. The strange effect of the brilliant flashing light was to show the audience how distorted Leontes's perception was. In 1981, despite the apparently jolly celebrations, Patrick Stewart's Leontes soon showed himself to be at odds with what was happening around him. His jealousy and his underlying neurosis was there from the beginning, as some have suggested they are meant to be, though it is not easy to support such an opinion from a close reading of the play.

A director has of course not only to decide what to do with Sicilia, but how to relate what he has done there to Bohemia. If Sicilia is in Scandinavia or fairly close to the Arctic Circle, where is Bohemia? In 1976 the answer was: still in Scandinavia but in summer. The dominant colour of the set had become warmer, there was a deal of festival jollity and Autolycus was portrayed with quite broad farce. The BBC television production, being unlocalized, was able to effect the change quite simply and preserve the overall consistency of style by putting down some artificial grass, making the stylized tree brown with some yellowish foliage, and lighting the set with warmer lights. In other productions jollity can be rural, Bohemian, and rather hard to date precisely. In 1960 it was extremely energetic, with lots of foot-stamping to music by Lennox Berkeley. Several critics thought it was like a fertility rite: some approved and others disapproved, but it was certainly one of the most remarkable things in the production, reminding us that romance is not the effete, pretty, pseudo-genteel thing it is sometimes taken for, but does have its roots in a vigorous, fertile, life-enhancing green world. These were certainly not 'young women doing eurythmics at Speech Days or on vicarage lawns' as Tillyard once complained they too often were. In 1981 it all took place at a Victorian village festival, which accorded with the period chosen for the court scenes in the first part, while contrasting in its informality with the formality of the court. A link between town and country was provided by Autolycus who was presented rather like a fugitive from the Music Halls, or perhaps a variety of fugitives, for he was forever adopting a new role, accent or disguise. In 1969 the contrast between the two kingdoms was not only one of place but of time as well. Bohemia was a land full of late 1960s hippies with long hair, beards, beads, extravagant fashions, vigorous music and energetic dancing. Of course many critics disliked the production and viewed it disparagingly as simply modern gimmickry. However, it did make a very striking contrast between the two places, especially in temporal terms – no one could doubt that a new generation had arrived.

The handling of the change from Sicily to Bohemia is difficult for a producer. There can be few plays in which the whole audience waits to see how one scene will be treated. In this play everyone knows about the bear. Often directors are nervous of the reaction to an attempt to make the bear realistic. If the bear aims at realism and fails will the effect be ludicrous and will every performance echo with unintentional laughter? How far, if at all, should the incident be presented as comic? Should the comic treatment be completely confined to the Clown's account which follows? Shadows and imaginings between light and dark were often the refuge of directors. Trevor Nunn in 1969, however, decided to have a realistic bear, but a huge one which lumbered across a stage lit once again by stroboscopic lighting, and it was a success with audiences and with many critics, too. In 1981 the shadow was back, huge, shrouded in mist, glimpsed only briefly and frighteningly before Antigonus was lost in utter darkness. It perhaps suggested the revenge of a great natural force on the albeit unwilling agent of human wickedness. In 1976 there was no attempt at a real animal, but an actor wearing a bear mask and carrying a staff with human skulls on it led, rather than chased, Antigonus off. He was presumably meant to represent death itself and a little later appeared as Time, so Antigonus's demise was, perhaps, seen as a function of time rather than representing something more portentous. On television the use of close-ups and cutting can avoid the difficulties of staging. In 1986 one might say the problem was 'swept under the carpet', or that this was the first Antigonus to be eaten by a rug. The huge polar bear rug that had been on stage during the first half of the play disappeared into a trench in the stage, and then towered up with flashing eyes to envelop Antigonus and carry him back into the same trench.

There is considerable variation in the presentation of the figure of

Time, too, though perhaps not so much difficulty. In 1986 at Stratford, Time literally flew, and this delighted the audience, though like many pieces of spectacular staging it may have distracted them from what he said. Time in the television production was presented, by contrast, in front of a plain background by an elderly figure clad in country clothes. In the 1960 Stratford production he was very different, an elegant and eloquent figure. There, as he spoke of Leontes, the king appeared behind him moving up-stage with courtiers, and then came Florizel with his falcon on his wrist gazing and circling round with Perdita. Time's words were made visible with a device that could be thought of either as looking back to the dumbshow (like that in *Pericles*), or as looking to the techniques of film and television presentation.

There are many incidents and scenes which one could describe and compare from different productions and, in considering our reaction to them and questioning or appreciating their effectiveness, we can frequently discover a great deal about the structure and the meanings of a play. We should set as wide an experience of seeing performances as we can against our critical reading of the text. If a novel asks to be read, a play has to be performed: that is the kind of work of art it is, and only in the theatre can it be fully realized.

6. Critical Views of the Play

Introductory

This chapter will attempt to give an account of the major critical views of *The Winter's Tale*. It will naturally give most space to more recent work. The reader may well feel that earlier accounts of the play are in any case only of interest as curiosities of critical history, and there always seems to be a positive antipathy to what is just out of fashion. But one should, perhaps, reflect that most followers of new approaches have felt that way about previous ones and that subsequently, when the process of reaction has died down, a careful reader can find much to think about in the observations of those whose conclusions he does not share.

Early reactions to the last plays, with the exception of *The Tempest*, which has been admired for its adherence to the unities by neo-classicists and for its appeal to the imagination by romantics, were quite often adverse. Ben Jonson is said to have ridiculed the presence of a Bohemian sea coast in *The Winter's Tale*, described *Pericles* as a 'mouldy tale' and had a generally disparaging view of romance drama. Dryden linked *The Winter's Tale* with *Pericles* and indeed 'many of the rest' as plays 'grounded on impossibilities' deriving from 'some ridiculous and incoherent story'. Pope doubted the authenticity of much of *The Winter's Tale*, as well as of *Love's Labour's Lost* and *Titus Andronicus*, and the whole of *Pericles*. Dr Johnson remarked on the 'unresisting imbecility' of *Cymbeline*. Charlotte Lennox even preferred the 'paltry story' (*Pandosto*) on which *The Winter's Tale* was based; William Warburton considered it 'monstrous', and Mrs Inchbald in 1822 thought it better 'in perusal than in representation' on the stage.

Of course the plays were not initially recognized as a group composed over a period of some five years at the end of Shakespeare's career, between 1607 and 1612. The critical practice of treating them together, which quite naturally persists, really became properly established only with Edward Dowden's *Shakespere: A Critical Study of his Mind and Art* first published in 1875. (For the results of more recent scholarship, Sir Edmund Chambers's *William Shakespeare: A Study of Facts and Problems*, (Oxford, 1930), and the section on 'Chronology and Sources' by G. Blakemore Evans in *The Riverside Shakespeare*, Boston, 1974, may be consulted.) One obvious, and indeed welcome and fruitful, consequence of this approach has been to stress the similarities between the plays. However, it should not be allowed to blur the differences, something which F. R. Leavis pointed out in his essay 'The Criticism of Shakespeare's Last Plays: A Caveat', first published in 1942. Likewise the view that these plays are very different from any of Shakespeare's earlier plays has been somewhat modified by a number of more recent critics who have written, for example, of Shakespeare's debt to romance throughout his career.

Dowden's view, shared by his contemporaries and immediate successors, was that these plays were the fruit of a period of terminal tranquillity, and were less accomplished than what had gone before. Both opinions, sometimes together and sometimes separately, have had many supporters over the years and have naturally provoked as many reactions. For example, Lytton Strachey in a celebrated and irreverent essay written in 1904, accepted that Shakespeare's artistic powers were diminishing, and pointing to the wickedness, violence and discord in the last plays, took issue with Dowden and his followers, suggesting that Shakespeare was torpid rather than serene, and was bored and filled with disgust by everything but his 'poetical dreams'.

However, no matter what their differences, these late nineteenth- and early twentieth-century critics approach their subject from what is essentially the same point of view. The plays, however important in themselves, are seen as indices of their writer's personality, and it is an image of Shakespeare the writer and the man, his moods, emotions and attitudes which emerges. Often it is an image of an ageing, even an old man, though he was only forty-six or forty-seven when he wrote *The Winter's Tale*, and of a man coping with, or relaxing in, retirement in the country. While this is no longer a popular critical approach, the vestiges lingered on for a long time; in 1925 E. K. Chambers suggested – perhaps imagined would be a better word to use – that after a breakdown Shakespeare recovered and saw the world as a well-ordered and tranquil place; Clifford Leech, writing in 1950, not only inclined to an unsympathetic view of Prospero not unlike Strachey's in some respects, but saw it as a reflection of the dramatist's own emotional condition.

Sometimes, most recently by Kenneth Muir, comparisons have been made with the last periods of other writers. This is rather different. It is not strictly biographical, but seems to start from the more general premise that all retired artists have something in common and that it can be seen reflected in their work. The other part of Strachey's argument, that Shakespeare's powers were in decline, is much less frequently supported now and the artistry of the plays more generally admired, though occasionally critics suggest that they are sometimes given more than their due.

Parabolic Readings of *The Winter's Tale*

There are probably more parabolic readings of the last plays – that is, readings treating them as saying one thing but meaning, implying or suggesting another, seeing them as symbolic, mythopoeic, anthropological or allegoric – than there are of any other kind. Like biographical criticism, these approaches once so popular and considered so exciting are now less favourably regarded. Historically their roots are in those approaches to classical religion and literature fashionable in Cambridge in the first half of this century which sought to penetrate beneath the surface and discover archetypal patterns and relationships with vegetation myths and fertility rituals. The major problem with this kind of criticism is that it tends to lead one further and further from the play. The deeper some critics delve beneath the surface, the more anything can be made to seem like anything else. If what becomes important is proving that everything boils down to the same fertility myth, the less they are aware of the individuality, the particularity, the uniqueness, of the work of art they sought to understand. To F. C. Tinkler writing in *Scrutiny* in 1937, the pattern of loss and restoration in *The Winter's Tale* was linked with the rhythm of the seasons and the spiritual health of the divine king. Florizel and Perdita are like 'vegetation deities' and in the final reunions and harmony the 'Waste Land' is restored to fertility.

One critic associated with this movement who has developed and elaborated myth criticism since the 1940s is Northrop Frye, and he stands head and shoulders above the rest. He, too, looks for deep structural patterns and motifs beneath the surface of the fiction. For example, in his essay 'The Argument of Comedy' (1949), and again in his influential *The Anatomy of Criticism* (1957), he put forward the view that 'the original nature-myth of Demeter and Proserpine' is clearly present behind the apparent death and revival of Hermione. Frye finds the same 'structural element' to be common in Shakespearean comedy (in *Much Ado About Nothing* and *Cymbeline* for example) and elsewhere, from Spenser to Dickens and beyond. While Frye is often no less reductive than his fellows in seeking to elucidate the significance of romance as a kind, he has aways taken Shakespeare's last plays very seriously as a 'genuine culmination' of his work. His argument has been developed over decades by restatement and elaboration, and although the reader may be frustrated and even irritated by his apparent unwillingness to engage often, or at any length, in specific analyses of individual plays, or with specific critics and their views, it is the disadvantage of taking that longer view of romance. He is always stimulating and provoking and his writing is full of fertile suggestions and insights, expressed with commendable pith and brevity. *A Natural Perspective* is to be recommended.

One thing Frye is not is an allegorist. He makes it quite clear in *A Natural Perspective* that *The Winter's Tale* is not an allegory, and in his edition of *The Tempest* makes the same point about that play, seeing it as neither an allegory nor a religious drama. Allegorical interpretations have, however, been approved of by many critics. There was a study of *The Tempest* in 1921 which treated it as a mystery play, and in 1950 F. D. Hoeniger stated that 'only if we approach *The Winter's Tale* as an allegory can we do justice to its greatness'. For him the play allegorizes a deep cultural pattern and reflects the myth of rebirth and immortality to be found in the vegetation cycle. He suggests parallels between Hermione and Perdita, and the classical expression of the myth in the story of Proserpina (Persephone) and her mother Ceres (Demeter); and his treatment of the concluding harmony speaks of Leontes achieving a paradise like the heavenly city of the New Testament, and of his reunion with Hermione as like that of Dante and Beatrice.

The most celebrated proponent of the view that Shakespeare's final plays were, as he called them, 'parables of a profound and glorious truth' and should be read as 'myths of immortality' was G. Wilson Knight (*The Crown of Life*, p. 30). His pioneering work, *Myth and Miracles*, first appeared in 1929 and again as part of *The Crown of Life* in 1947. His style is vigorous and urgent and the argument drives on apace. According to Wilson Knight the fundamental and unchangeable verities about God, man and nature expressed in common symbolic language are found in myth, ritual and art: 'Art is an extraverted expression of the creative imagination which, when introverted, becomes religion.' While he thought that 'Shakespeare's . . . poetry corroborates the death-conquest announced by Christianity', his criticism was not explicitly Christian – 'all my comparisons of Shakespeare and Christianity assume a preliminary recognition of their difference' – and he denied any simple 'doctrinal and dogmatic orthodoxy' (p. 31). In *The Winter's Tale* he observed, like many others of his persuasion, 'a strong suggestion throughout of season-myth, with a balance of summer against winter'. Here 'maturity and death are set against birth and resurrection' (p. 76), while 'Leontes, under the tutelage of the Oracle . . . painfully [works] himself from the bondage of sin and remorse into the freedom of nature.'

The Christian analogy was replaced in the work of S. L. Bethell with an explicitly Christian interpretation of *The Winter's Tale*, published in book form in 1947 and developed in an edition of the play in 1956. He defended himself against adverse criticism by asking, with some justice, whether it was only 'the churchman whose judgement is warped by his beliefs' (*The Winter's Tale*, p. 12), and whether some critics were convinced that 'Shakespeare cannot have seriously held the dogmas of Christianity . . . because their own humanist way of thinking has become so natural to them that they mistake its dogmas for the laws of nature and think that all well-disposed persons must be of their party' (p. 13). Bethell's own position is quite clear: 'my concern is with expressed beliefs and unconscious attitudes, and all my reading of the plays has gone to confirm my opinion that Shakespeare wrote consistently from the standpoint of orthodox Christianity' (p. 14). By the end of the book he was able to write: 'I think it is not too much to claim that the play represents an important moment in the history of Christian civilization' (p. 118). But at least Bethell was aware of his own prejudices, allowing that when we read 'each of us will tend to be impressed by an aspect related to his own interests. If we have Shakespeare the botanist, and Shakespeare the horse-leech, why not Shakespeare the theologian?' (p. 13). Though Bethell's main thesis has been viewed with considerable scepticism over the years, his work contains many good ideas and acute observations. For example, he deals well with the self-conscious fictionality of the play, commenting on the rejection of realism, the use of 'naïve' romance sources and 'apparently crude and incoherent' dramatic techniques, and he has many interesting observations on style and characterization.

D. Traversi was one of the few critics of this, or indeed of any, persuasion who seemed to prefer *The Winter's Tale* to the other last plays. He reads the play, as he reads all the last plays, as symbolic, as an 'expanded image'. A persistent theme in these plays was, he considered, the stress on the need for a balanced relationship between natural simplicity and civilized life, both as a social necessity and as an aspect of the maturity of the individual. It all sounds relatively sensible and safe, which may be why his work was once very popular and influential, when symbolic readings were the prevailing fashion.

In fact, with most of the symbolic interpretations, the meaning mysteriously shadowed in the play turns out to be not at all profound but simply rather dull. However seductive their approach is, such a lot seems to be lost in translating the symbols that one is frequently left asking, with justifiable disbelief, when a sophisticated and subtle work of art has been reduced to its 'meaning' – 'was it all for this?' Interestingly, Frye provides a corrective for his own school – 'the meaning of the play is the play, there is nothing to be abstracted from the total experience of the play' (*A Natural Perspective*, p. 116) – and Frank Kermode, who had suggested that *The Tempest* might be seen as an 'exposition of the themes of Fall and Redemption' by 'analogous narrative' (Arden, p. lxxxiii), wrote a few years later in his short but good pamphlet on the last plays: 'The greatness of the play is self-evident, it does not need the prestige of covert meanings' (p. 37).

Alternative Critical Approaches

When E. M. W. Tillyard published his *Shakespeare's Last Plays* in 1938, despite repeated gestures towards the prevailing symbolic interpretation of the plays, and a thesis which is finally unsatisfactory, there are several signposts to future critical developments. Tillyard saw the plays as developing out of the tragedies, indeed completing what he considered to be the proper tragic pattern by including a final necessary stage of regeneration which was only suggested in the tragedies themselves. Actually, only *The Winter's Tale* could really be made to fit his scheme of 'prosperity, destruction and recreation' with any real plausibility. However, his view of the plays as an integral part of a developing *œuvre*, rather than a completely new, even eccentric, departure was valuable; and he was also in the vanguard of those critics who have since stressed the importance of understanding romance conventions as a preliminary to an understanding of the play.

Since the 1950s a number of books have taken this as their starting point and have detailed the elements from this tradition: the vigorous non-naturalistic, incident-packed narrative, the coincidences, surprises, disguises, the separation of parents and children, ignorance of birth, shipwrecks, wild beasts, love, danger, escapes from disaster by the skin of the teeth, apparent deaths and incredible restorations, and so on. The classic pioneering study by S. L. Wolff relating Elizabethan prose fiction to the Greek romance included observations on Shakespeare's debt to the tradition, and more recent work has been done specifically on Shakespeare by Carol Gesner. Her book helpfully provides an account of the romances and their influence on earlier works before turning to Shakespeare. She suggests that the alterations Shakespeare made to *Pandosto* are in the tradition of Greek romance and, as Wolff had done before her, that *Daphnis and Chloe* was a source for the pastoral in *The Winter's Tale*. However, when it comes to critical interpretation she belongs to an old school, suggesting that the use of romance contributes to making a 'symbolic interpretation of character and events' possible. J. F. Danby and E. C. Pettet, amongst others, remind us of the importance of Sidney's *Arcadia*, and Pettet stresses the fascination romance held for Shakespeare as source material throughout his career: more evidence that the last plays are firmly rooted in his earlier work. The introductions to the Arden editions of the other last plays, as well as the one to *The Winter's Tale*, have also given space to accounts of romance influence in general as well as in relation to the play in question.

Studies of *The Winter's Tale* frequently begin by comparing it with *Pandosto*. G. Bullough's helpful introduction to the texts he prints in his *Narrative and Dramatic Sources of Shakespeare* naturally comments on Shakespeare's alterations, and this is where John Lawlor's essay (reprinted in *Shakespeare's Later Comedies*) begins and also, even more interestingly, Stanley Wells's essay 'Shakespeare and Romance' in *Stratford-upon-Avon Studies* VIII. Wells observes, for example, that there is greater personal responsibility for events in Shakespeare, and examines the nature of the play's realism and lack of realism in comparison with Greene's work. Fitzroy Pyle also founds many of his observations on comparisons: his is a quite detailed and useful commentary.

Hallet Smith's excellent book, *Shakespeare's Romances*, starts with chapters on romance and pastoral and aims to show that Shakespeare is returning in his romances to something popular in his youth, and that 'the romances are a natural outgrowth of his experience in writing comedy and tragedy', which, as he observes, at least as far as comedy is concerned, is an aim similar to that of Northrop Frye in *A Natural Perspective*. However, his 'Appendix A: Myth, Symbol and Poetry', which is headed by an epigraph from *A Midsummer Night's Dream*: 'How easy is a bush supposed a bear!', sharply demonstrates that he has no time for symbolic criticism; nor has he any time for the kind which seeks to identify topical allusions or occasions for the plays (Appendix B). I have not devoted any space in this summary to the latter because I, too, find the suggestion that the play may be seen as figuring a 'mystical marriage of Prince Henry (Florizel) to the three kingdoms', whose lost unity represented by Perdita has been recovered by Time and King James, no less unbelievable than he does. Those wishing to weigh the case for themselves should consult the two pieces by Glynne Wickham listed in the bibliography.

David Young in *The Heart's Forest* approaches a discussion of the structure of *The Winter's Tale* from the pastoral tradition, and compares the pastoral elements in *As You Like It*, *King Lear*, and *The Tempest*. There are many interesting comments not only on pastoral but also on the structure of the play, the handling of tragic and comic elements, time, the presentation of character and much else.

B. Mowat's book *The Dramaturgy of Shakespeare's Romances* is also worth consulting. She writes interestingly on styles and modes. C. Frey's *Shakespeare's Vast Romance* is full of material, including an analysis of the play, a discussion of critical views and some stage history. While his work does not break new ground, he makes some worthwhile observations. He also gives an account of what his ideal production of the opening scenes should be like.

Over recent years critics have often turned to a consideration of works in performance. This was the title of John Russell Brown's book in 1966, *Shakespeare's Plays in Performance*. In it he considers, among other things, the effect of theatrical performances on audiences, citing evidence from accounts of productions in earlier times, and also discusses the few opportunities there are of 'playing for laughs' in the last plays. There have also been discussions of certain scenes and the sort of reaction they produce, for example by N. Coghill, 'Six Points of Stage-craft in *The Winter's Tale*'; and by W. H. Matchett, 'Some Dramatic Techniques in *The Winter's Tale*'. Richard Proudfoot has written of the way in which producing the play made him particularly conscious of verbal reminiscences between the two halves. R. P. Draper's volume on the play in the *Text and Performance* series gives considerable space to questions of direction and performance, using recent productions as examples. A comprehensive account of the stage history of the play and of performances up to 1976 is to be found in Dennis Bartholomeusz, *The Winter's Tale in Performance*.

From the early years of this century the relationship between the late plays and current theatrical fashions, especially as they were reflected in the work of Shakespeare's younger contemporaries Beaumont and Fletcher, has been the subject of critical interest. It was once suggested that Shakespeare was adopting and developing an interest in romantic tragicomedy which they had begun to make popular. However, more recently the view has been that some of the influence may have been by, rather than on, Shakespeare. Much has depended on speculative dating. Even the similarities between his plays and those of his contemporaries do not seem quite so extensive to all readers as was once suggested. There is certainly no longer thought to be so sharp a division between the late plays and his earlier work, but the ideas about dramatic structure and effect may be shown to have developed gradually. Shakespeare's place in the theatre and art of his day is an interesting subject and comparisons with his contemporaries are often very illuminating, though before influence may be established hard evidence is needed. Care should be taken, here as everywhere else, to recognize more fanciful speculations for what they are.

A great deal of work has been done on the Elizabethan and Jacobean theatre itself and is still very much in progress. Here scholarly arguments, contentions, theories and speculations still abound. Those who wish to know more may read Andrew Gurr's *The Shakespearean Stage 1574–1642* – the second edition of which (1980) has a very useful select bibliography – before consulting, if necessary, the monumental (but now sometimes superseded or modified) reference works by E. K. Chambers and by G. E. Bentley.

G. E. Bentley suggested in his essay 'Shakespeare and the Blackfriars Theatre', that the plays were planned specifically to suit the new theatre at Blackfriars acquired by the King's Men in summer 1608. This was a small, artificially lit, private theatre with a different kind of audience which would, it was suggested, have had different expectations from that in the public theatre. Bentley argued that to cater for this the company employed Jonson, Beaumont and Fletcher, all with experience of the private theatre, and that Shakespeare, both alone and in collaboration with Fletcher, turned to writing a different kind of play. There are a number of problems with his argument, attractive though it is; for example *Pericles*, a very obvious romance, had already been written and given at the Globe before the company took over Blackfriars. Scholars have also doubted that the two audiences had such different tastes, or that the plays were especially appropriate to one theatre rather than the other, given what is known about performances.

Probably no simple, single reason is to be found to explain the nature of these late works. It is much more plausible to suggest that all these elements may have had some effect on the dramatist. Two stages, one of them rather different from the other; an abiding interest in developing the potentiality of dramatic form, and an awareness of the technical innovations of others; different current interests in romance, which had been drawn on by Shakespeare throughout the course of his career: all these may help to account for something of the nature of the last plays. But neither one nor all of them can be said to 'explain' Shakespeare's art. Like the symbolic readings these 'explanations' can be reductive. Whatever the elements upon which he wrought his alchemy, it is to the product of their transmutation, to the plays that we must always return.

Bibliography

Texts of *The Winter's Tale*

The edition of *The Winter's Tale* used throughout and to which all references are made is the New Penguin edition, edited by E. Schanzer. This has a good introduction and commentary. The New Arden edition, edited by J. H. Pafford in 1963, is also very useful and has a longer introduction, a more extensive commentary, a section on stage history and includes *Pandosto* in an appendix. The introduction in the Signet edition, edited by F. Kermode also in 1963, is interesting. S. L. Bethell edited the New Clarendon edition in 1956 and this includes and extends views first published in his short book on the play. The New Cambridge edition of 1931 is not important, and is only worth consulting as a curiosity: a new edition is in progress. The New Variorum edited by H. H. Furness in 1898 is also being redone but, as it stands, it still gives the most comprehensive collection of eighteenth- and nineteenth-century annotations to the play, and gives quite full accounts of earlier critical attitudes, performances and adaptations of the play.

E. Schanzer (ed.), *The Winter's Tale*, New Penguin Shakespeare (Harmondsworth, 1969).

J. H. Pafford (ed.), *The Winter's Tale*, Arden Shakespeare (London, 1963).

F. Kermode (ed.), *The Winter's Tale*, Signet Classic Shakespeare (New York, 1963).

S. L. Bethell (ed.), *The Winter's Tale*, New Clarendon Shakespeare (Oxford, 1956).

H. H. Furness (ed.), *The Winter's Tale*, New Variorum Shakespeare (Philadelphia, 1898).

Critical Studies of *The Winter's Tale* and Other Last Plays

C. L. Barber, '"Thou that beget'st him that did thee beget": Transformation in *Pericles* and *The Winter's Tale*', in *Shakespeare Survey*, XXII (1969).

D. Bartholomeusz, *The Winter's Tale in Performance in England and America, 1611–1976* (Cambridge, 1982).

A. Barton (ed.), *The Tempest*, New Penguin Shakespeare (Harmondsworth, 1968).

G. E. Bentley, 'Shakespeare and the Blackfriars Theatre' in *Shakespeare Survey*, I (1948).

S. L. Bethell, *The Winter's Tale* (London, 1949).

J. R. Brown, 'Laughter in the Last Plays' in *Stratford-upon-Avon Studies*, VIII (1966).

J. R. Brown and B. Harris (eds), 'Later Shakespeare', in *Stratford-upon-Avon Studies*, VIII (1966).

N. Coghill, 'Six Points of Stage-Craft in *The Winter's Tale*' in *Shakespeare Survey*, XI (1958).

L. S. Cox, 'The Role of Autolycus in *The Winter's Tale*' in *Studies in English Literature*, IX (1969).

R. P. Draper, *The Winter's Tale: Text and Performance* (London, 1985).

P. Edwards (ed.), *Pericles*, New Penguin Shakespeare (Harmondsworth, 1976).

P. Edwards, 'Shakespeare's Romances: 1900–57' in *Shakespeare Survey*, XI (1958).

I. Ewbank, 'The Triumph of Time in *The Winter's Tale*' in *Review of English Literature*, V (1964).

H. Felperin, *Shakespearean Romance* (Princeton, 1972).

C. Frey, *Shakespeare's Vast Romance: A Study of The Winter's Tale* (Columbia and London, 1980).

N. Frye, *A Natural Perspective: The Development of Shakespearean Comedy and Romance* (London, 1965).

N. Frye, 'Recognition in *The Winter's Tale*' in *Essays on Shakespeare and Elizabethan Drama: In Honor of Hardin Craig* (Columbia, Missouri, 1962).

J. Hartwig, 'The Tragicomic Perspective of *The Winter's Tale*' in *English Literary History* XXXVII (1970).

F. D. Hoeniger, 'The Meaning of *The Winter's Tale*' in *University of Toronto Quarterly*, XX (1950).

F. D. Hoeniger (ed.), *Pericles*, Arden Shakespeare (London, 1963).

F. D. Hoeniger 'Shakespeare's Romances Since 1958: A Retrospect' in *Shakespeare Survey*, XXIX (1976).

D. G. James, 'The Failure of the Ballad Makers' in *Scepticism and Poetry* (London, 1937).

F. Kermode (ed.), *The Tempest*, Arden Shakespeare (London, 1954).

Critical Studies: The Winter's Tale

F. Kermode, *Shakespeare: The Final Plays* (*Writers and Their Work*, No. 155, London, 1963).
G. Wilson Knight, *The Crown of Life* (London, 1947).
M. Lascelles, 'Shakespeare's Pastoral Comedy' in *More Talking of Shakespeare*, ed. J. Garrett (London, 1959).
F. R. Leavis, 'The Criticism of Shakespeare's Late Plays: A Caveat' in *The Common Pursuit* (London, 1952; Peregrine, 1962).
D. A. Male, *Shakespeare on Stage: The Winter's Tale* (Cambridge, 1984).
W. H. Matchett, 'Some Dramatic Techniques in *The Winter's Tale*' in *Shakespeare Survey*, XXII (1969).
B. A. Mowat, *The Dramaturgy of Shakespeare's Romances* (Athens, Georgia, 1976).
K. Muir (ed.), *The Winter's Tale: A Casebook* (London, 1968).
K. Muir, *Last Periods of Shakespeare, Racine, Ibsen* (Liverpool, 1961).
J. M. Nosworthy (ed.), *Cymbeline*, Arden Shakespeare (London, 1955).
A.D. Nuttall, *Shakespeare: The Winter's Tale* (London, 1966).
D. J. Palmer (ed.), *Shakespeare's Later Comedies: An Anthology of Modern Criticism* (Harmondsworth, 1971).
D. L. Peterson, *Time, Tide and Tempest: A Study of Shakespeare's Romances* (San Marino, California, 1973).
E. C. Pettet, *Shakespeare and the Romance Tradition* (London, 1949, 1970).
R. Proudfoot, 'Verbal Reminiscence and the Two-part Structure of *The Winter's Tale*' in *Shakespeare Survey*, XXIX (1976).
F. Pyle, *The Winter's Tale: A Commentary on the Structure* (London, 1969).
E. Schanzer, 'The Structural Pattern of *The Winter's Tale*' in *Review of English Literature*, V, ii (1964).
D. Seltzer, 'The Staging of the Last Plays' in *Later Shakespeare, Stratford-upon-Avon Studies*, VIII (1966).
P. N. Siegal, 'Leontes a Jealous Tyrant' in *Review of English Studies*, I, iv (1950).
H. Smith, *Shakespeare's Romances: A Study of Some Ways of the Imagination* (San Marino, California, 1972).
J. Smith, 'The Language of Leontes', *Shakespeare Quarterly*, XIX (1968).
L. Strachey, 'Shakespeare's Final Period' in *Independent Review*, III (1904).
R. Studting, 'Spectacle and Masque in *The Winter's Tale*', in *English Miscellany*, XXI (1970).

E. M. W. Tillyard, *Shakespeare's Last Plays* (London, 1938).
F. C. Tinkler, '*The Winter's Tale*' in *Scrutiny*, V (1937).
D. A. Traversi, *Shakespeare: The Last Phase* (London, 1954).
S. Wells, 'Shakespeare and Romance' in *Later Shakespeare, Stratford-upon-Avon Studies*, VIII (1966).
R. S. White, *Shakespeare and the Romance Ending* (Newcastle-upon-Tyne, 1981).
G. Wickham, '*The Winter's Tale*: A Comedy with Deaths' in *Shakespeare's Dramatic Heritage* (London, 1925).
H. S. Wilson, 'Nature and Art in *The Winter's Tale*' in *Shakespeare Association Bulletin*, XVIII (1943).
ibid., 'Shakespeare's Investiture Play: The Occasion and Subject of *The Winter's Tale*', *The Times Literary Supplement*, 18 December 1969.
A. F. Yates, *Shakespeare's Last Plays: A New Approach* (London, 1975).
D. P. Young, *The Heart's Forest: A Study of Shakespeare's Pastoral Plays* (New Haven, 1972).

Background Material

F. Bacon, *The Essayes or Counsels*, ed. M. Kiernan (Oxford, 1985).
C. L. Barber, *Shakespeare's Festive Comedy* (Princeton, 1959).
G. Beer, *The Romance* (London, 1970).
G. E. Bentley, *Shakespeare: A Biographical Handbook* (New Haven, 1961).
G. E. Bentley, *The Jacobean and Caroline Stage*, 7 volumes (Oxford, 1941–68).
M. C. Bradbrook, *The Growth and Structure of Elizabethan Comedy* (London, 1955).
A. C. Bradley, *Shakespearean Tragedy* (London, 1904).
G. Bullough (ed.), *Narrative and Dramatic Sources of Shakespeare*, 8 volumes (London, 1957–75).
T. Campion, *Works*, ed. P. Vivian (Oxford, 1909).
B. Castiglione, *The Book of the Courtier*, trans. T. Hoby, ed. W. Raleigh (London, 1900).
E. K. Chambers, *The Elizabethan Stage*, 4 volumes (Oxford, 1923).
E. K. Chambers, *Shakespeare: A Survey* (London, 1925).
E. K. Chambers, *William Shakespeare: A Study of Facts and Problems*, 2 volumes (Oxford, 1930).
P. Crutwell, *The Shakespearean Moment and Its Place in the Poetry of the Seventeenth Century* (London, 1954).

J. F. Danby, *Poets on Fortune's Hill: Studies in Sidney, Shakespeare, Beaumont and Fletcher* (London, 1952).
M. Doran, *Endeavors of Art* (Madison, Wisconsin, 1954).
E. Dowden, *Shakespeare: A Critical Study of his Mind and Art* (London, 1875).
T. Elyot, *The Book Named The Governour*, ed. H. S. Croft, 2 volumes (London, 1880).
G. B. Evans, 'Chronology and Sources' in *The Riverside Shakespeare*, ed. G. B. Evans (Boston, 1974).
B. Ford (ed.), *The New Pelican Guide to English Literature 2: The Age of Shakespeare* (Harmondsworth, 1982).
N. Frye, 'The Argument of Comedy' in *English Institute Essays 1948* (New York, 1959).
C. Gesner, *Shakespeare and the Greek Romance* (Lexington, Kentucky, 1970).
W. W. Greg, *Pastoral Poetry and Pastoral Drama* (London, 1906).
A. J. Gurr, *The Shakespearean Stage, 1574–1642* (Cambridge, 1970; revised 1980).
F. E. Halliday, *A Shakespeare Companion* (London, 1952).
D. L. Hirst, *Tragicomedy* (London, 1984).
C. W. Hodges, *The Globe Restored* (London, 1953; revised 1968).
C. W. Hodges, *Shakespeare's Second Globe* (London, 1973).
E. Jones, *Scenic Form in Shakespeare* (Oxford, 1971).
B. Jonson, *Works*, ed. C. H. Herford, P. and E. Simpson, 11 volumes (Oxford, 1925–51).
C. Leech, *Shakespeare's Tragedies and Other Studies in Seventeenth-century Drama* (London, 1950).
C. Leech, *Tragedy* (London, 1969).
Longus, *Daphnis and Chloe*, trans. P. Turner (Harmondsworth, 1968).
M. M. Mahood, *Shakespeare's Wordplay* (London, 1957).
M. Merchant, *Comedy* (London, 1972).
M. de Montaigne, *The Essayes*, trans. J. Florio, ed. C. Whibley (London, 1905).
J. de Montemayor, *Diana*, trans. B. Yong, ed. J. M. Kennedy (Oxford, 1968).
K. Muir, *Shakespeare's Sources* (London, 1957; revised 1977).
K. Muir and S. Schoenbaum (eds.), *A New Companion to Shakespeare Studies* (Cambridge, 1970).
K. Newman, *Shakespeare's Rhetoric of Comic Character* (London, 1985).
A. D. Nuttall, *A New Mimesis: Shakespeare and the Representation of Reality* (London, 1983).

Ovid, *The Metamorphoses*, trans. A. Golding, ed. W. H. D. Rowse, *Shakespeare's Ovid* (London, 1904).

F. H. Ristine, *English Tragicomedy: Its Origin and History* (New York, 1910).

L. G. Salingar, *Shakespeare and the Traditions of Comedy* (Cambridge, 1974).

S. Schoenbaum, *Shakespeare's Lives* (Oxford, 1970).

S. Schoenbaum, *William Shakespeare: A Documentary Life* (Oxford, 1975).

E. Spenser, *The Faerie Queene*, ed. C. P. O'Donnell (Harmondsworth, 1978).

S. Wells (ed.), *Shakespeare: Select Bibliographical Guides* (London, 1973).

S. L. Wolff, *The Greek Romances in Elizabethan Prose Fiction* (New York, 1912).

PENGUIN LITERARY CRITICISM

The English Novel Walter Allen

In this 'refreshingly alert' (*The Times Literary Supplement*) landmark panorama of English fiction, the development of the novel is traced from *Pilgrim's Progress* to Joyce and Lawrence.

Film as Film V. F. Perkins

Acknowledging the unique qualities of cinema as essentially a bastard medium – neither purely a visual nor a dramatic art – this pioneering text remains 'one of the most sophisticated and commendable works of film criticism' – *Tribune*

The Anatomy of Criticism Northrop Frye

'Here is a book fundamental enough to be entitled *Principia Critica*,' wrote one critic. Northrop Frye's seminal masterpiece was the first work to argue for the status of literary criticism as a science: a true discipline whose techniques and approaches could systematically – and beneficially – be evaluated, quantified and categorized.

The Modern World Ten Great Writers Malcolm Bradbury

From Conrad to Kafka, from Proust to Pirandello, Professor Bradbury provides a fresh introduction to ten influential writers of the modern age and the Modernist movement. Each, in their individual way, followed Ezra Pound's famous dictum – 'Make it new'.

Art and Literature Sigmund Freud

Volume 14 of the *Penguin Freud Library* contains Freud's major essays on Leonardo, Dostoyevsky and Michelangelo, plus shorter pieces on Shakespeare, the nature of creativity and much more.

The Literature of the United States Marcus Cunliffe

'Still the best short history [of American literature] ... written with notable critical tact' – Warner Berthoff. 'Cunliffe retains the happy faculty (which he shares with Edmund Wilson) of reading familiar books with fresh eyes and of writing in an engaging style' – Howard Mumford Jones

PENGUIN LITERARY CRITICISM

A Lover's Discourse Roland Barthes

'*A Lover's Discourse* ... may be the most detailed, painstaking anatomy of desire we are ever likely to see or need again ... The book is an ecstatic celebration of love and language and ... readers interested in either or both ... will enjoy savouring its rich and dark delights' – *Washington Post Book World*

The New Pelican Guide to English Literature Boris Ford (ed.)

The indispensable critical guide to English and American literature in nine volumes, erudite yet accessible. From the ages of Chaucer and Shakespeare, via Georgian satirists and Victorian social critics, to the leading writers of the 1980s, all literary life is here.

The Theatre of the Absurd Martin Esslin

This classic study of the dramatists of the Absurd examines the origins, nature and future of a movement whose significance has transcended the bounds of the stage and influenced the whole intellectual climate of our time.

The Theory of the Modern Stage Eric Bentley (ed.)

In this anthology Artaud, Brecht, Stanislavski and other great theatrical theorists reveal the ideas underlying their productions and point to the possibilities of the modern theatre.

Introducing Shakespeare G. B. Harrison

An excellent popular introduction to Shakespeare – the legend, the (tantalizingly ill-recorded) life and the work – in the context of his times: theatrical rivalry, literary piracy, the famous performance of *Richard II* in support of Essex, and the fire which finally destroyed the Globe.

Aspects of the Novel E. M. Forster

'I say that I have never met this kind of perspicacity in literary criticism before. I could quote scores of examples of startling excellence' – Arnold Bennett. Originating in a course of lectures given at Cambridge, *Aspects of the Novel* is full of E. M. Forster's habitual wit, wisdom and freshness of approach.